Breaking The Bou

The Rug Hooking Artistry of Sharon Johnston

Judy
TAYLOR

Sharon
JOHNSTON

Elizabeth
HERBERT

Acknowledgements

This has been quite the journey for me in the arts. Working in various mediums has expanded how I work today. I keep on the road of discovery as I experiment with traditional needlework that I can adapt to rug hooking.

Judy Taylor, I am honoured that you wanted to do this book and thank you for your continuing interest and support.

Thank you to my husband and daughters, who have been understanding and supportive and put up with my need to be creative. They give me the space and time to make art.

Thank you to Elizabeth Herbert, who wrote the foreword for this book, and others who have purchased pieces and supported me. All of you keep me inspired.

Thank you to Romana Kasper-Kraft of the Collectors Gallery for representing me and helping to promote rug hooking as ART.

Thank you to Paula Laverty and R. John Howe for sharing the history of rug hooking in Canada.

To all you fellow hookers, I hope this book opens new avenues for you. Books like this are what have taught and inspired me. May you continue to enjoy this traditional Fibre Art form.

If you wish to purchase any of my work it is available through collectorsgalleryofart.com.

Sharon Johnston, Calgary, Alberta

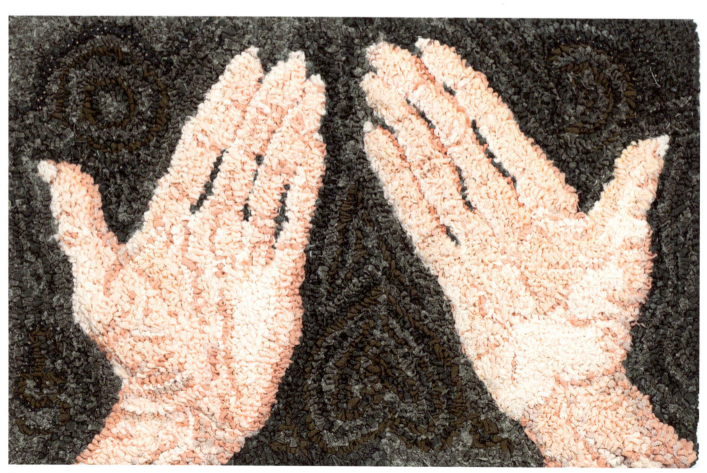

Table of Contents

FOREWORD............................... page 4	THE LADY & THE UNICORN....... page 101
INTRODUCTION........................... page 13	ABSTRACTS & GEOMETRICS..... page 107
FLOWERS................................ page 27	OF A COMMON THREAD.............. page 114
TREES & THINGS...................... page 35	CUSHIONS & BAGS...................... page 122
THE ELEMENTS........................ page 44	PROJECTS................................... page 135
SHOES...................................... page 50	ALPHABET BLOCKS..................... page 137
ANIMALS & BIRDS..................... page 64	IVY THE SHEEP............................ page 149
PEOPLE.................................... page 75	MISCHIEF..................................... page 182
DAYS OF CHILDHOOD............... page 84	TRAPUNTO SUNFLOWER............ page 196
PICTORIALS............................. page 92	HOBBIT HOUSE............................ page 216

Through a Woman's Eyes (above), 4.5" x 11"
Cotton fabric and eyelash yarn, with trapunto.

By A Woman's Hands (left), 9"x14"
Assorted cotton fabrics, light trapunto on a foam core.
For the Women's Hands Building a Nation travelling exhibit.

© 2021 Little House Books
ISBN 978-0-9976712-4-7
PO Box 2003
Auburn, WA 98071
www.littlehouserugs.com

FOREWORD

THE ART OF SHARON JOHNSTON by Elizabeth Herbert

There is a persistently humble quality about hooked rugs. Historically, they are associated with cast-off burlap feed bags, rags, and the thrums--leftover fibers from the productions of weaving mills. These materials at the dead end of utility signified purposes served, tasks completed, and processes finished. Women of little means were the gleaners of such remnants from factory floors and feedlots. The normal lifespan of a bolt of cloth, from the fancy petticoat to the bottom of the kitchen wash bucket, was prolonged and given a new purpose by the quick hands that collected fabric remains for the handwork needed at home. Often referred to as the "craft of poverty," rug hooking was a necessity rather than a pastime.

Single Polar Bear on Ice Pan, 26.5"x40.5" Design in production c. 1930, silk or rayon, brin, and cotton, dyed. Photo courtesy of Paula Laverty, from her book *Silk Stocking Mats, Hooked Mats of the Grenfell Mission*, 2005.

In Canada, the establishment of the Grenfell Mission (later Grenfell Industrial) in Newfoundland at the end of the 19c gave rise to a handicraft industry based on rug hooking. There, it was but one of a group of endeavours planned to improve the lives of precariously employed deep sea fishermen. Born again through necessity, hooked rugs made there were an industrialized transformation of what was originally a local aboriginal craft.

Under supervision, brilliant colors and innovative designs were abolished, and quality controls instituted. Soon, however, these Grenfell mats began to reflect the creative inspirations and visual intelligence of the artists themselves. Grenfell mats are characterized by unique combinations of mundane objects, local flora and fauna, and designs taken from old book plates. Today, such rugs command large prices, and draw the admiring attention of art writers and gallery owners.

For more information on Paula Laverty's extensive research on the Grenfell Mission, check out this post from R. John Howe: Textiles and Text (https://rjohnhowe.wordpress.com/2010/04/13/paula-laverty-on-grenfell-hooked-rugs/) and her website: http://www.grenfellhookedmats.com.

The career of Calgary fiber artist Sharon Johnston is a microcosm of the history of rug-hooking. As a result of the formative influence of necessity – Johnston's early life offered few opportunities for an intelligent and creative child – she was raised to ask for little and to "make do." As she recalls, "We were always hemming bolts of unbleached, unfinished cotton, and we got fabric ends by the pound. We made things out of other things."

Her maternal grandfather had been a Bernardo child - one of 35,000 young emigres from British orphanages and workhouses that were brought to Canada via a charitable institution founded by the preacher Thomas John Bernardo (1845-1905). One of seven children, her mother grew up in Surrey, British Columbia, and raised her own children there. After high school, Sharon (nee Fox), found a job at the Royal Bank in Burnaby, B.C. and at age 18, defiantly eloped with Dennis Johnston. They moved around northern BC doing construction work, then settled on a farm at Cache Creek where they raised their two daughters Leah and Manda. Sharon worked at a small jewelry store that was a tourist stop for visitors to the Canadian outback from Europe. Like all intellectually curious people, she sought interesting conversation at every opportunity. The store owners' son was a student of languages, and Johnston was informally exposed to a wide variety of people from different cultures.

She made jewelry, small crafts, painted, and even enrolled in a rug-hooking class, where she was promptly put off by the instructor's rigid, unimaginative instructional style and narrow view of the craft: "It did not appeal to me. There were way too many rules!" Like the early hooked rug makers, Johnston had always chosen her own materials from her immediate environment, and created objects from personal inspiration, rather than from pedagogical direction. Naturally, she determined to learn more about the craft of rug hooking by herself: "Some photos in a book caught my eye…and reading more about the subject, I decided to give it another try."

Johnston's focus on the creative potential of small things; fallen feathers, the corrugated bark of a tree stump, a curling leaf, or the glitter of a brass button, often leads directly to the generation of forms in her art. "Organic," and "Time Lines," are good examples of this process.

Time Lines (above), 33"x35.5"
Assorted yarns, pulled to assorted heights. From a photo where the cut branches on the old cottonwood looked like a face.

Organic (left), 25.5" diameter
Assorted yarns, from a photo Sharon took of a log end. She used pixelating to mix colors. 2nd in section 1st in class Calgary Stampede Arts & Crafts 2011 and in 2012, part of an emerging artist show, Western Showcase, Calgary Stampede.

On the other hand, the composition of "Boomtown" is a clearly laid out pattern combining linear perspective with a playful and abstracted stacking of groups of elements. Like Medieval art, it relies on the viewer's understanding that a vertical (higher or lower) placement on the picture stands in for idea that some things are farther away than others. Here the strong, blocky numerals embedded into the whimsical waves of the Bow river bring the eye firmly back to the surface of the image, and to the contemplation of its title and subject.

Boomtown, 24"x25"
Mixed yarns. The theme for the Calgary Stampede 2012 was spirit of 1912 for 100 years of Stampede. 1st in class 2nd in section Arts & Crafts. Her son-in-law helped with the design as he grew up in Calgary.

Interestingly, the most intrinsically natural forms in Johnston's art, like the spiralling water in "Whirlpool" are also the most abstract. "Sticks and Leaves," "Ammonite," "Fiddleheads," and "Fossils" are simultaneously records of intense observation, and technical invention. Conversely, Johnston's exuberant incorporation of "real" objects, "realistically placed" into her work catalyzes our experience of the vividly concrete and tactile nature of the medium. Never do her hooked rugs seem more like rugs than when they are astonishingly transformed into something else.

Whirlpool, 16.5"x22"
Cotton, velvet and satin, some trapunto on a foam core

Ammonite, 15"x16"
Satin strips on rug warp, stuffed and sewn with black yarn on foam core

Fossils, 13"x13"
Ribbon, cord and assorted fabric on foam core

Sticks and Leaves, 9.5"x18"
Yarn, yarn wrap, layered leaves on linen

Fiddleheads, 12"x16"
Yarns on linen, framed

This, of course, was the aim of Modernist painting, which in the estimation of the French Symbolist painter Maurice Denis was an arrangement of lines and colors before it was "a warhorse" (or a scene from a honky-tonk saloon in Dawson City, Yukon during the Goldrush). Ladies of the Night was inspired by Johnston's reading of "The Harpy," a poem from *Songs of a Sourdough* by Robert Service, published in 1907. The Harpy is an entertainer of men, and a denizen of low places. Fallen, scarlet, and aflame with fury, she declares in stanza three of the poem:

I paint my cheeks, for they are white,
And cheeks of chalk men hate;
Mine eyes with wine I make them shine,
That man may seek and sate;
With overhead a lamp of red
I sit me down and wait

At the expressive and compositional heart of the image is a figure resplendent in a crimson dress. Her feathers and ribbons, twinkling jewels and bravado ruffles are at once part of the iconography, and the real world of the viewer. They are, like the fringes of the buckskin jacket worn by an admiring customer on the far left, both literally themselves, and imaginary. The red lamps establish focal points on either side of the heroine and boundaries at the vertical and lateral edges of the work, which is softly irregular, like a pelt, or a document darkened and scarred at the edges by handling and history.

Ladies of the Night, 23"x34"
Assorted fabrics, yarn and leather, feathers, some embroidery and embellishments, trapunto.

Barn Dance, 26.5"x29" Assorted fabrics and yarn, designed from memory of square dancing at a past Stampede. 1st in class, 2nd in section 2016 Calgary Stampede Arts & Crafts

In the marvelous Barn Dance, the detailed view of an interior scene is further developed. Here there are strong framing elements; a banjo, a pair of cowboy boots, and an actual horseshoe fastened to the upper left corner. In a way reminiscent of the conventions of turn of the century postcards, this enframement of an actual scene by using related thematic images serves to emphasize the artifice of the image as a whole. To paraphrase René Magritte, we are thus reminded that this is not a barn dance, it is a picture of a barn dance. Like the postcard, it is a souvenir – a reminder of days gone by. Five couples whirl and swing into a loosely elliptical group in the foreground of a raucous, wholesome and delightfully uninhibited scene. Brilliant, saturated primary colours are transformed from skirts to shell and bell shapes by gusts of air following the women's dance movements.

The lady in the red skirt is a tour de force of expressive characterization; she extends one long, bony white arm into a downturned wrist that signals both coyness and exuberance, as she recoils ever so slightly from her eager partner. The weathered barnwood plank floor recedes not via a predictable linear perspective, but rather rises up like flanking ocean swells, to vertiginous effect. It cradles the central group of dancers, and tips them ever closer together. The niche above the dance floor, the hayloft of the barn, is populated by gnomelike musicians and a dance caller, who is perched, like the guitar player to her right precisely along the linear edge of the platform, as if to challenge any illusion of three dimensionality. As in Boomtown, the vivid text affixed to the upper wall is both a title and an assertion of the essential flatness of the fiber surface.

Similar pictorial devices are used in Birds of a Feather Flock Together, a meeting of suffragette ladies seen through a church window. Presented from the shoulders up, like so many animated and vivacious busts, their gazes are fixed on one another. Feminist solidarity is further emphasized by the words, "WE ARE PERSONS" woven almost invisibly between the four large heads aligned like guardians across the bottom edge of the composition. To see these solemn words, we must pay attention. Here, the subject is the prelude to the famous petition to the British Privy Council by five Canadian women in 1929, which asserted the right of female adults to hold public office. These are indeed women of character; their dress collars and eyebrows are boldly defined, and the dark elaborate hat of the third figure from the left emerges from her head like a fortress, leading the eye upward through the crowd, toward the pinnacle of the window itself. Johnston's iconography is historically authentic. Among her sources was a contemporary catalogue of women's clothing from the Hudson Bay Company, and plates from a book about the history of their hats. "It was a time in women's history I find interesting considering the rules of the times and dominance of males," Johnston explains.

Birds of a Feather Flock Together, 24"x26," on linen with assorted fabrics and feathers, trapunto.

Johnston's most ambitious work to date is the group of 27 heads, collectively titled Of a Common Thread. They were exhibited in a travelling group show titled Womens' Hands Building a Nation, celebrating the contributions of women to Canada on its 150th anniversary, at the Galleria in Calgary in 2017. They were the subject of a solo exhibition at the Edge Gallery later that year. Johnston describes them as " representing different waves of immigration to Canada…we have all come from somewhere to settle this land…(they) are in cloth and yarns using new and old techniques, hence another common thread."

pure black, and the highlights with irregular patches of mixed grey, purple and brown to convey both the true undertones of the skin, and the impression of light reflecting from it. Her head is a combination of a profile and three quarters view; while we see the silhouette of her features, we see also both of her eyes. The lifted brows and liquidity of the gaze create an impression of vulnerability and sensitivity. A subtle black outline around the headdress suggests recession into depth, and thus mass and volume. From a small, flat woven mat a personality emerges, and claims her space.

The Englishwoman is a feisty, aging rose. The neat blue hat, augmented by a "real" ribbon contrasts with a fair face gently marked by a multitude of age spots, and a small dark mole above her left eyebrow. The area of the chin, and within the boundaries of the na-so-labial folds is lightened to suggest emergence from the plane of her cheeks, and she looks out at us with a discerning (if not judgemental) blue eye.

In this work of multiple elements a thematic and aesthetic unity is achieved. The painterly qualities of each complexion are created through a complex interweaving of color areas and textures. The vibrant lemon yellow of the Sudanese woman's clothing reflects light by way of strategically placed sections of sepia, cream and buff. On the face, matte sections are worked with

In true Johnstonian style, the Inuit woman is nestled within a fluffy white aureole of real fur. The delicate monolid eyes are expressively cast sideways, and her heart shaped lips appear to have parted slightly in response to something she sees.

With the exception of the Aboriginal women, all of these people are immigrants, and on the threshold of a strange new world. These are individuals, but are characterized by their culture of origin. They have converged through forces of chance and history, and again through the creative imagination of their maker.

Johnston's working method encapsulated prior approaches and incorporated some new ones. "I researched all the countries I included on the internet, in books on national costumes and head dress, as I would only be using heads and a bit of shoulders. I tried to choose a national look for each and sometimes I just played with the look because I liked a certain hat. Then I made quick sketches and saved photos and scans to work from for colours. I saved eyes for shape and colour, and other features for the different nationalities. I then drew out each in the size I wanted and traced those onto the backing fabric. I proceeded to hook and add embellishments to give a more ethnic look to each. Showing the heads spurred me on as an artist and the feedback I received gave me confidence to push the tradition further."

(You can view the entire collection "Of A Common Thread" on page 114.)

The relationship between rug-hooking and the handwork of women has been well established. For some contemporary artists, the medium's strong historical associations are subverted to expressive effect. However, Johnston's work expresses an affiliative and personal feminism which is shaped by her own history, and a ferociously independent turn of mind. She does not readily receive the wisdoms issuing from either end of the political spectrum, and continues to nurture ideas through the wisdom of her own hands.

Elizabeth Herbert received an M.A. in Art History from the School of Oriental and African Studies (University of London, U.K.) and an M.A. from The Courtauld Institute of Art (UnivCuersity of London, U.K.). She was a Lecturer in art history at University of Calgary for many years, and worked as a Curator and Museum Educator at the Glenbow Museum in Calgary.

Curator of exhibitions:
The Lithography of John Snow and Maxwell Bates, Nickel Arts Museum, University of Calgary 2011
The Art of Marion Nicoll, A Retrospective, Nickel Arts Museum, University of Calgary 2013
Goddesses of Tooth and Breast: The Female Divine in Hinduism, Art Gallery of Alberta, Edmonton 2019

Publications
The Art of John Snow (U. of Calgary Press) 2011
The Art of Marion Nicoll (U. of Calgary Press) 2013

She is currently at work on a book about the artist H.G. Glyde. She is also a qualified English as a second language teacher, and has taught literacy courses to immigrant women in Calgary. She is currently tutoring children in Language Arts and Social Studies. She has 3 adult children and lives with a Violet-Naped Lory parrot, a cockatiel, a standard Poodle named Louis, and a Havanese puppy named Fergus.

INTRODUCTION

Communications, 22"x41." Assorted cotton fabrics. Sharon used plastic bags to hook the phones, then she took photographs of phone screens, printed them on fabric and painted them with glue to make them shiny!

I have known Sharon Johnston for many years. I say "known," although we have never met, nor even talked on the phone! I have admired her work for a long time, included her rugs in one of my books, my blog, website, and Rug Hooking Daily. Her work stands out for me. There is always something that attracts my attention, but until we embarked on this book project, I couldn't say what exactly drew my eye to her rugs. Boy, did I get an education!

The impetus for starting this book came from a series she did last year called "Seasons." It depicts the four seasons, as experienced through the changing weather. It was beautiful, certainly, but there was something about this series that wouldn't let me go. I kept thinking about those rugs, wondering how she did them.

They are rug hooking, yes, but they are so much more. They represent to me a fantasy world, an idyllic place, and her clever use of perspective draws me in, as if to say, "You wanna take a walk?"

I was mesmerized by the trees, the writhing roots, the undulating branches. Those leaves and that mossy ground. They looked so natural and lifelike.

Spurred on by the need to know more, I boldly asked her if she would consider collaborating on a book project with me. She said yes! What followed was about 300 photos, more than could ever be included in a single book, a flurry of emails, questions, answers, which led to more questions… Pretty soon, we had a real book on our hands (now in yours).

I bet you'd like to see the Seasons series right about now (they are on the next few pages). Let's just take a moment and really study them. Notice the materials and effects she used; wrapping the trees around cording creating a 3-D effect, her assortment of materials used to create texture, and her use of embroidery and proddy to highlight details. The pieces are not large (mostly 12"x18"), which makes her shading and perspective even more impressive.

Spring in the Woods, 12"x18." Assorted yarns, wrapped cord, embroidery, prodded felt leaves.

Summer in the Woods, 12"x19." Assorted yarns, wrapped cord, embroidery, prodded felt leaves.

Autumn in the Woods, 12"x18." Assorted yarns, wrapped cord, embroidery.

Winter in the Woods, 12"x 19." Assorted yarns, wrapped cord, embroidery.

It was clear to us at the start that we weren't going to be able to teach Sharon's artistic style, which is broad and varied. That would take several books. But we settled on five signature techniques that she has developed, which make her work unique and special; uneven edges, reverse hooking, trapunto, layering and wrapping. As you will see, these techniques can be added to any style of rug hooking. We've developed five projects that you can try at the end of the book. Once you try them, if you're like me, your mind will go straight to, "How can I incorporate this method into my next project?"

Sharon has always done art of some sort; drawing, painting, batik, fabric painting, pottery, collage, sewing, quilting, embroidery, weaving, knitting, crochet... you get the idea. I think a lot of fiber artists dabble in other media, which enriches their artistry. But when she discovered rug hooking, all her artistic instincts fell into place and found expression.

At first glance, you might think this was a painting, it's actually a collage made of tissue paper!

Butterfly Quilt using trapunto

Batik (above), Woven scarf (below)

Rug hooking didn't take right away for her, though. She attended a class in 2000 but found the traditional method of rug hooking too confining. She was allergic to wool, first off, so she began to experiment with other materials. Rug hooking for her was a jumping off point, a leap to create something totally new.

A sampler piece experimenting with 26 different materials

Techniques demonstrated in this book:

1. Uneven edges
2. Reverse hooking
3. Trapunto
4. Layering
5. Wrapping

The wonderful thing about rug hooking is that it is totally individual. No two people approach rug hooking in quite the same way. If every one of us sat down and hooked the same pattern, our finished rugs would look totally different. We each have our own palette, the colors we are most drawn to. We interpret design differently, adding special touches to make it our own. Some of us create rugs with wool fabric strips, others branch out, hooking with yarn, T-shirt strips and other materials. Whenever I see a hooked rug, the first think I think is, "Who made it?"

The techniques we will be demonstrating in the book are mainly for wall hangings and decorative items. It would be difficult to use her uneven edges in a floor rug, because it would be hard to protect the backing from wear and tear. And the other methods, reverse hooking, trapunto, layering and wrapping create a 3-D effect, so are not recommended for floor rugs (we might trip on them!).

In my thirty years of rug hooking, my main goal has been durability. Part of my business is repairing old hooked rugs (older than me, even!). I want my rugs to last for generations as well, which means I choose certain colors, patterns and finishing techniques intended for hard wearing rugs. I have made wall hangings too, of course, but they look like rugs hanging on the wall. Now that I have sampled Sharon's techniques, I feel like a whole world of artistic possibilities has opened up for me. When you remove the question of durability, your artistic choices are unlimited. A wall hanging is plenty durable though, and will last even longer than a rug on the floor.

If you think about it, we only have so much floor space in our homes. We have around four times that in wall space, if you count decorating our interior doors. Suddenly, the walls in my home are looking blank and empty to me, soon to be filled with rug hooking. What a marvel that now I can create any kind of edge, I can texture, sculpt and embellish my work, I can freely use light and bright colors and unusual textiles. Just try and stop me now!

Sharon's work has been displayed and sold in art galleries all over Alberta and Saskatchewan. Many of her projects that you'll see in this book are available to purchase. She never makes the same thing twice. She doesn't sell patterns or kits, because every piece is serendipitous.

Sharon isn't a dyer, she's a *finder*. She's a treasure hunter, who sees the possibilities in textiles you and I would walk right past, without a second glance. No wonder she doesn't attempt to reproduce her designs.

All of Sharon's work is protected by copyright and is included here as a source of inspiration. However, the projects in the end of the book are free for you to use, enlarge, and alter to suit your own taste.

Unless otherwise indicated, all projects in the book are Sharon's creations. I could have put "Designed and hooked by Sharon Johnston" 300-plus times, but that would lead to carpel tunnel, and I don't know about you, but I would much rather hook than type.

Samples:
Wool, wool blends, polar fleece, flannelette, cotton, cotton blends, terry cloth, denim and other twills, polyesters, silks, shiny and sparkly fabrics (although use sparingly as they pop!), velvet, velour, satin lining material, T-shirt material, nylons, knits, yarns, also chamois, light leathers and fur. You can't use a cutter, cut with scissors, but don't worry about width. Experiment with high loops and low loops. Experiment with cutting along the warp, or across the grain. Avoid loose weave fabrics. Consider both sides of the fabric, sometimes you can do shading with different sides.

An organized work space makes the process easier. Finish what you start before moving on to the next piece. You will be more efficient and feel more creative. If you are experimenting, make small pieces that you can finish and keep for reference. Once you get in the habit of following certain principles, they come automatically.

There are few rules, and rules are made to be broken, so experiment!

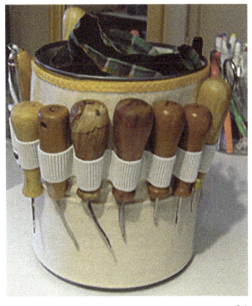

I keep a box full of odds and ends for using as embellishments. I pick up little things in craft stores that maybe sometime I can use. Leaves, sticks, feathers, shells, bark, rocks, wild plants for dried bouquets, these make excellent reference material.

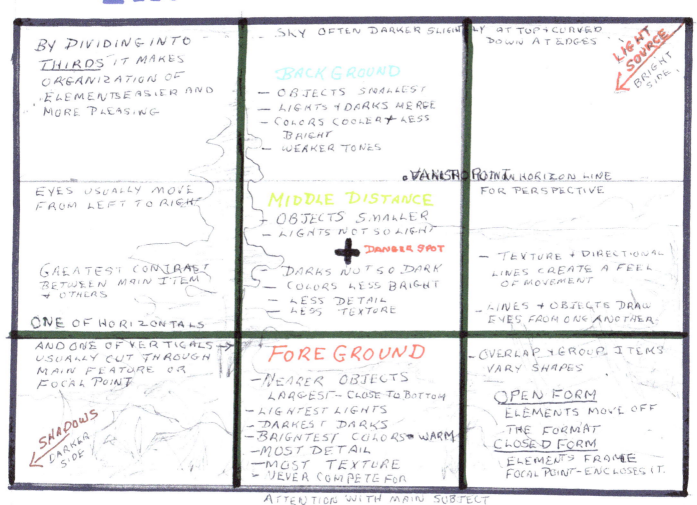

When planning a realistic design, your backing fabric should have your border marked out and then light direction marked with an arrow in one corner. I like to mark the exact centre so I don't make the mistake of putting my centre of interest there. Divide the piece into thirds which makes it easier to place things, laying out your foreground, middle and background, if you're trying to create distance. Keep in mind moving colour around for the eye to follow as well as lines and textures. Perspective is important, too.

Color planning for the Gandalf Rug

Here you can see some of the fabrics and yarns Sharon has gathered to use in her Gandalf Rug. She needs a wide variety of shade, color, texture and thickness on hand, so she can experiment with the details. As the hooking continues, her confidence grows.

Trying an alternative method might lead you to a process that has some intriguing outcomes.

Copying another textile artist will not make your work look like theirs. You are a unique individual, so why would you want to? Discover your own creativity using all the tools, materials, and knowledge you have.

Gandalf (in progress), 11"x15." Assorted fabrics and yarn.

Our practice projects are intended mainly for intermediate rug hookers. It's not that the techniques themselves are difficult, but there was no space in this book to cover the basics, like how to hook with yarn, fabrics strips or other materials, how to transfer your design to the backing, to frame or not to frame, etc. I have listed some of my other books in the back which cover all the basics. Once you have a few hooked projects under your belt, you'll be ready to try the ones in this book.

Years ago, I attended a class called "Freeform Crochet." If you've never heard of the craft, it's pretty much how it sounds. Using crochet (and knitting) stitches, you wander about, creating odd shapes called "scrumbles," which you connect together in an inifinite variety of possibilities and combinations. It was a perfectly delightful class, my main takeaway from which was whenever a student would ask a question, the teacher's answer was always the same: "Yes, you can."

"Can I use two different colors of yarn at the same time?"

"Yes, you can."

"Can I use ribbon or lace?"

"Yes, you can."

"Can I create three dimensional effects?"

(Say it with me now) "Yes, you can."

That's how I feel about Sharon Johnston's work. It's totally liberating. There are few rules, and nobody can tell you what's right or wrong. You are the master of your own creations.

But before we get to practicing her signature techniques, let's take a tour through the gallery of her work. Put your feet up, take your time, bring a snack. Focus on the details. Remind yourself that Sharon doesn't dye, she finds the colors she needs. And remember too, that many of her projects are relatively small, which makes detail and shading even more challenging. Enjoy the tour, and we'll meet again on the other side.

F L O W E R S

Flowers play a large part in nature's reproduction, Nature's most colourful bounty. The first flowers of spring lift our spirit, they are a bright and happy sight and a symbol of hope. Through the ages they have been given special meanings and there is a whole 'language of flowers.' They play a large part in our lives and culture. We either give or receive flowers on special occasions and they are a part of many of our ceremonies. A garden of flowers or a hillside in bloom are a joy to behold.

White Daisies, 10"x22." Cotton fabric and yarn. The centers of the flowers were hooked with yarn, high loops that were trimmed to shape. The background was hooked with patterned fabric.

Tiger Lilies, 12.5" x 18.5." Cotton fabrics and some embroidery.

Resilience, 7.3"x9.8." Sharon used roving and clipped it to make the fluffy parts. For the flower, she clipped some petals and not others. *This shows what a messy hooker I am but it gives me some results I would not get if I was to work in neat orderly way.*

Bill's Sunflowers
10" x 15"
Cotton fabrics.

Flower sampler 12" x 15." This was an experimental piece on cheap burlap, hooked with mostly cotton or cotton blends fabric. The large flower was prodded with center hooked and cut. Some of the other flowers are hooked and cut. For the basket, various sized strips were woven through backing. There is some daisy stitch embroidery and the background was painted last with acrylic paint.

Iris Again,
9" x 15."
Assorted fabrics
and yarn.

Blanket Flower, 9" x 12." Cotton and misc. fabrics.

Remembrance Poppy, 11" x 19." Velvet, satin and other fabrics, embroidered center.

TREES & THINGS

Trees are nature's lungs with each having its own unique shape and pattern. They clean our air and are a big part of the ecosystem. They provide all kinds of habitats for insects, birds and animals. Trees provide shade, food and wood for our homes.

They have become a motif in many cultures such as the Tree of Life. Many of our stories and fables have trees in them. The rings of the tree record life. Just as the branches become stronger, as they reach for the sky, we grow stronger in knowledge and experiences. Trees are one of our most important species.

Woodland Slices, 26"x35." Yarns, hooked at various heights. *It sets out different stages of tree life. The background blocks represent building and pulling together to make a whole.*

Just as with Organic and Time Lines (page 6), Sharon has long been fascinated by nature, forever drawn by textures and colors.

Even though there is decay, there is still beauty in it. There is an orderliness to it all, and mystery in the cracks, splits and dark areas. Since rings tell the age of a tree, its age is also seen in the deep furrows and creases in the bark, much like our own age lines that become more pronounced with time. The raised ridge in Time Lines (page 6) around the cut is like a scar and tells of healing.

Squirrel on a Stump

Squirrel 9" x 10." Yarn, fancy yarn tail, stuffed, bead eye & claws. A magnet on bottom holds him on stump.

Stump is 10" in diameter 14" high. Assorted yarns over plastic flower pot, roots are cord wrapped with yarn, and the base is 30" across. Hooked with assorted yarns. A magnet was fixed on top of the flower pot to hold squirrel. Part of the woodland series.

As I worked this piece, I wanted to show the roots of an old tree stump. It seemed empty so I added the black squirrel. The whole work was challenging, as I attempted to create a full-sized dimensional piece, mostly with yarns.

My Neigbours Tree, 9" x 15.75." Cotton tree, satin sky. Notice 3 hidden birds on branches.

I see textures, lines and colours within each subject, then marry them with yarns or fibres to represent them. Trees and plants invite us to tap into their energy and the relationships within nature and our own lives. We see the magic of Nature and its designs, and the world that surrounds us becomes a more intricate part of our lives.

(right) This is an experimental piece with hooking natural grasses etc. It is about 4" square on cheap burlap.

(opposite page) Small Tree for Mandy, 5"x7." Yarns, wrapped trees.

39

Pine Cone, 10' x13." Cotton fabrics, trapunto under the cone, attached to foam board.

In this half-rounded piece, I wanted to show an old tree with its preserved scar. I wonder who carved it, when and why. Perhaps they were lover's initials, or someone saying 'I was here.'

Woodland Slices 26" x 35."
Assorted yarns, some wrapping.

Autumn Carpet, 22.5"x 26." Mostly cottons and yarns, part of Sharon's woodland series. Sticks and Leaves (page 7) was part of this series as well and was done about same time. *Walking through the leaves made me think nature was laying a carpet to keep things warm through winter. This colourful carpet would gradually become more dull as the leaves decayed. Yet we could enjoy their beauty for a short time with each leaf being unique and yet being a part of the whole carpet. Working on this piece also gave me an opportunity to try "trapunto," a technique of raising an area by stuffing and quilting it. This gave a more dimensional feel to the piece.*

Lone Tree, 14"x22." Assorted yarns.

THE ELEMENTS

Mother Earth, 11"x13." Mostly cotton fabrics, trapunto on foam board.

The Earth is a symbol of all life. It stabilizes, anchors, reuintes and re-establishes all things in an order of balance. Earth provides a solid foundation with fertile abundance for the millions of species inhabiting it. Our planet Earth is ever changing and all species continue to evolve within its changing physical environment.

The third planet from the sun, Earth harbours life on its solid surface, of which 70% is water. Without the connection of Water and Air, the Earth would lose its nurturing value. The densest planet with a powerful magnetic field, it once was believed to be the centre of the universe and solar system. Often referred to as Mother Earth, it embodies the concept of home and belonging.

We don't think much about Air. We literally take the element into ourselves with each breath. Air is essential to our survival, it represents the breath of life, the flow of energy. Breathing is your life's voice reflecting mood by its depth, smoothness, rate and sound.

Air is a light, changable element that moves. It has many forms, each can affect our moods, calming or energizing. The Air can be calm, cold, warm, damp, dry, dusty or stormy, moving on the wind. We all know how quickly the wind can change.

Air molecules surround us, and carry sound as well as movement. Our atmosphere, the never-ending sky, wind, clouds and sounds carried to our ears, is all due to Air. It affects us so greatly, yet we hardly give air a thought.

Clean Air, 10.75" x15.5." Mostly cotton fabrics, trapunto on foam board.

Water makes up 70% of our earth surface with only 3% being fresh and potable, the other 97% is found in oceans and is too saline for human use.

Water is life, which in turn, is mainly composed of water. We are wholly dependant on Water for the survival of all life forms. In our personal lives, it determines where we live and our quality of life. Water provides transport of nutrients and waste within our bodies and enables reproduction for humans and other species and plants. Without Water, soft tissue shrivels as would the earth's surface.

We use water in many ways; from transportation, sanitation, irrigation, energy and cooling, and much more. It provides food production, processing, manufacturing, transport and recreation. With water being our most valuable resource, the consequences are far reaching and devastating when we waste, misuse and misappropriate water.

Water is a visible cycle, maintaining the ecological balance. Clouds collect water and drop that moisture, allowing soil to soften, for without water, soil is lifeless. Growth helps hold moisture. Clouds also provide a buffer from the sun and stabilizes temperatures that aid growth. The earth collects water which is picked up by the wind and forms new clouds so the cycle continues.

Water is taken for granted by mankind and carelessly and extravagantly used. It would be a terrible shame to lose our precious Water through neglect.

Precious Water, 10" x15." Mostly cotton fabrics, trapunto on foam board. Plastic bags hooked for the water.

Fire lives in the belly of the earth. It needs earth-based matter to spark or originate. Fire is a source of energy that requires moderation and control. Combined with Air energy, Fire is combustive and consumes, but not without giving back light, warmth, and active energy.

Control of Fire by early humans was a turning point in human evolution. It provided warmth, protection from predators, methods of cooking food and creating more advanced tools as well as a longer waking day. This laid the groundwork for human society and made it possible for other products of culture, language and form. Cooking food made it possible for the human body and brain to evolve into what we are today. In taming Fire, we have set off our evolutionary path and there is no turning back.

Fire, 10 "'x15.5." Mostly cotton fabrics, trapunto on foam board.

SHOES

In 2018, Collector's Gallery of Art featured Sharon Johnston's Shoes Series, called *Journeys.* Sharon told me, "I got the idea when we were throwing out some old shoes. They had so much character I decided to photo and hook them. Then I started researching the history of shoes and friends gave me old shoes to photo and laces when they heard what I was doing and I just kept going. My daughter Manda started to photo and organize the hooked shoes and then we decided to make a book on them and do little write ups on the history of each."

This section is excerpted from Sharon's book on her gallery show.

Journeys by Sharon Johnston is a series of worn shoes, hooked in various fabrics, yarn, leather and plastic wrap. They've been hooked on rug warp, then quilted and stuffed with cotton fill for dimension.

Why shoes?

Most people walk 100,000 miles (160,934 km) in a lifetime. Shoes provide protection, improve performance and serve as tools appropriate to the occupation and job.

Right and left shoes came into being around 1850. Whether they are objects of ornamentation or utilitarian, they are symbols of the time. They express not only gender and sexuality but also ethnicity, status, profession, politics and freedom.

Shoes have a role in fairy tales, stories, myths and superstitions. Footwear is the foundation of every outfit and is a large part of fashion trends. Every culture has their own style of shoes which change with the trends, times and places they are worn. The connotations of shoes are powerful, magical and life changing.

Every pair of shoes has a fascinating story to tell about the time, land and climate in which they are worn. Shoes possess a unique narrative that concerns routes they took in becoming part of someone's life, the paths they followed, the people who wore them: a history.

JOURNEYS
Sharon Johnston

Baby Shoes

The first baby shoes have sentimental value and are often saved and bronzed. Crafted for boys and girls from soft white leather, they stabilize the baby's feet when they first start walking.

Mary Janes

Children's bar or T-bar shoes are secured with a strap over the instep and fastened with a buckle or button and were worn by both sexes.

Their name comes from the shoes worn by a character "Mary Jane" in the comic strip *Buster Brown* in 1920. Little girls everywhere were asking for them in colors other than the usual black patent, with red being considered the most feminine. Many characters in movies and cartoons were seen wearing them. They became mostly a girls shoe and were popular with women in 1920s as dance shoes.

Converse Runners

The American Converse Rubber Shoe Company began manufacturing shoes in 1908. The company's long history was highlighted by a high-topped black canvas shoe with rubber sole, designed for basketball players. Its iconic style with the "All-Star" patch on the side continues to endure despite the demise of the original company. Today it has re-emerged with the same shoe's design, but is now favored as a vintage style.

Running Shoes

These shoes came into being in 1917 and were advertised as an athletic shoe. Later they were called sneakers because of the rubber sole; they could sneak around silently. The sneaker started out as a prestigious shoe for the upper-middle class with a desire to impress their status during leisure activities.

Male Work Shoe

The working man's shoe has evolved from a need for a sturdy, durable and comfortable shoe. They often look similar to an Oxford or running shoe and are made of leather, with chunky rounded toes and heavy, durable treaded soles. Work shoes often have protective features such as steel toes and other impact guards. Their style is usually limited to basics such as black, brown or grey.

Work Boots

Work boots are made with durable materials and often have steel toes for protection. They are worn for their functionality, protection and support. Their strong masculine implication is why small boys like to try to wear their dad's work boots.

53

Men's Dress Shoes

This men's indoor shoe of plain leather has become a popular dress and professional shoe. The lace-up design is efficient and comfortable with the Oxford being the most common option with many variations of style. The Brogue was originally designed as a field shoe. With its sporty decorative perforations along the toe cap it has since become a popular dress and business shoe.

Military Boots

The traditional black military boot has in modern times become part of the formal military uniform in many countries. Military or combat boots now vary in color, materials and design to suit varying climates and military environments. They have also been adapted for civilian use.

Slip-ons or Chelsea Boots

Chelsea boots were the first of their kind to utilize a fabric or elastic panel that allowed the wearer to slip boots on and off easily. They have a long tradition stemming from Victorian times and have seen many variants and changes since. Their popularity was strengthened during the 1960s British rock and roll culture.

Wellingtons

The rubber Wellington boot is based on early leather military riding boots. Vulcanized rubber was introduced in 1852 and the rubber Wellington was manufacured shortly thereafter. The rubber is hardwearing, comfortable and waterproof. They have quickly become a staple in agriculture, fishing, hunting and outdoor activities. The British traditional green version is still worn today, despite the many colours now available and is favored by the British aristocracy and royal family.

Police Boots

Law enforcement boots are styled to be authoritive and are often black. They are comfortable, quick to put on and easy to take off, and protect the body from harm in different situations. This ride style boot is worn by officers riding motorcycles or on mounted patrols.

Mules

This shoe style is backless, making them easy to slip on and off. These shoes come in various styles, heel height and materials. Mules originally were a sexy bedroom slipper and the style was favored by Hollywood pin-ups. Today this shoe is typically an indoor slipper and outdoor shoe for both sexes.

High Heels

High heels have gone through numerous phases during their long and eventful history. A heeled slip-on shoe with a low cut front was called a "court" shoe, "pompe" or pump. Pumps showcased wealth and status and eventually became the object of widespread female fashion. Today they are worn from work place to evening wear and even casually.

Cowboy Boots

Cowboy boots refer to a specific style of boot historically worn by cowboys. They have a Cuban angled heel over one inch high with a pointed toe and high shaft without lacing. The boot has a smooth sole, tall heel and slightly pointed toe ideal for inserting into the stirrup. The tall leather shaft provides protection to the leg and should easily slip off if a rider is in danger of being dragged by the horse. Leathers and decorative details vary widely and have been influenced by the Wild West shows and movies.

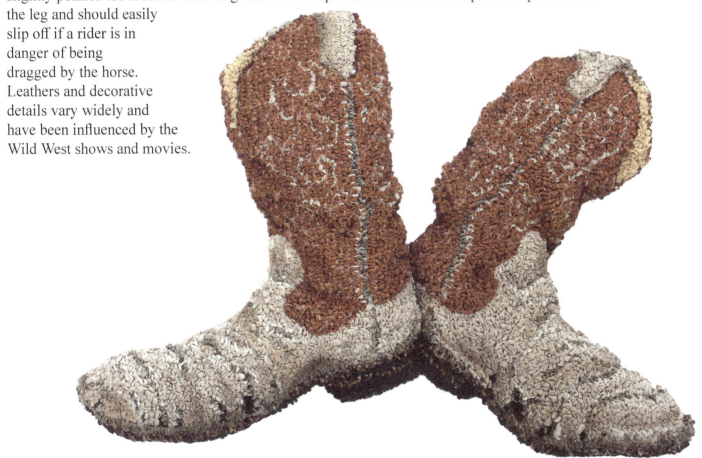

Ballet Shoes

For the past 150 years, ballet (or pointe) shoes have changed little. They look delicate but provide support for the dancer's feet while dancing on point (standing on their toes). They are mostly made from satin with the box toe of paper, canvas and glue, and the partial sole remaining thin and inconspicuous as possible. They are expensive and hardly last beyond one performance.

Ladies Flat Shoes

The ladies flat shoe or ballet flat was traditionally worn by women and men as a court shoe in medieval times. Today they continue to be worn by women in work, casual and evening occasions. Film stars of the 1950s made them both sensible and sexy.

Flip-Flops

Over centuries a huge variety of cultures utilized sandals made from a variety of materials. Flip-flops got their name from the sound they make when walking. Modern flip-flops gained popularity after World War II. Worldwide, people of all ages choose flip-flops because they are cheap and easy to take on and off. The flip-flop is mostly worn in warm climates and are made of rubber, leather and sometimes pretty trimmings.

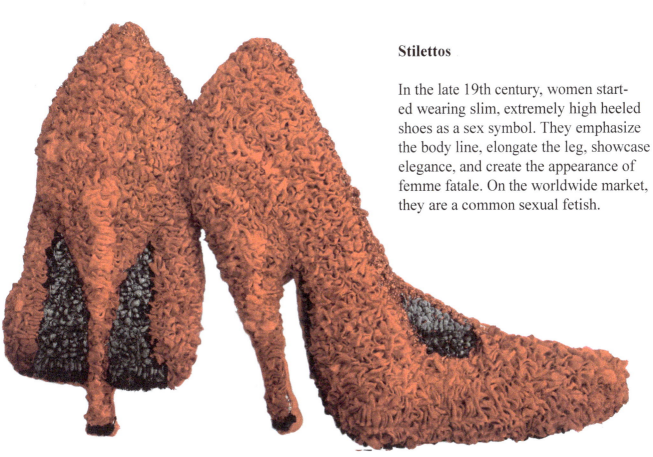

Stilettos

In the late 19th century, women started wearing slim, extremely high heeled shoes as a sex symbol. They emphasize the body line, elongate the leg, showcase elegance, and create the appearance of femme fatale. On the worldwide market, they are a common sexual fetish.

Nurse Shoes

Nurses' pristine white uniform attire was the traditional standard for many years. The difficult task of maintaining this fresh and clean appearance was made even more difficult when white leather replaced traditional black shoes. Nursing shoes sported a heel and a pinpoint textured pattern, making them cumbersome to maintain and uncomfortable after long work hours. Nursing shoes have evolved to provide supportive comfort, offer many styles and are no longer limited to white.

Leather Clogs

These wooden sole shoes have a leather strap or straps that wrap over the top of the foot and are attached to the sole. Clogs vary with culture but basically have remained unchanged and are used worldwide. In Europe, the clog was durable, cheap footwear that became the most common work shoe throughout the Industrial Revolution.

Mukluks

These soft boots traditionally made by First Nations
People from animal hides,
created warmth and maneu-
verability in natural environments. Mukluks today
are styled similar to original
versions and have become
popular winter footwear.

Moccasins

Moccasins are footwear
created by First Nations
People. Flexible and soft,
they allowed the wearer
to move about the land
quietly. The style, pattern
and decoration of mocca-
sins indicated the wearer's
clan or community. Moc-
casins are a popular indoor
shoe today with many shoe
styles derived from them.
They are often lined with
fur for greater warmth and
are made from various
animal hides.

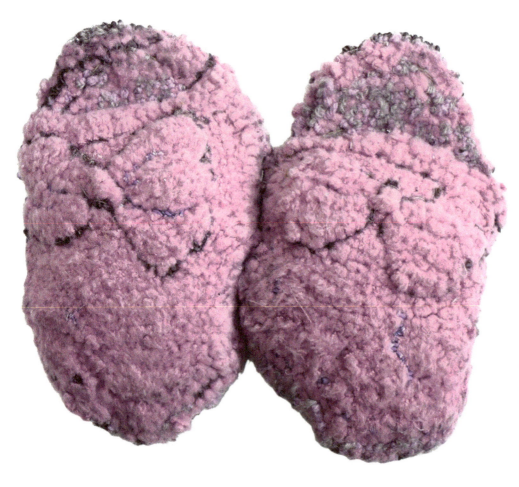

Slippers

It is thought that the slipper originated in the East, but have been worn by every culture. They are soft with thin soles for indoor use. This made them a captivity shoe of harems. Slippers range from women's more elaborate styles to fluffy children cartoon characters and men's slippers called Grandads. The more time we spend indoors, the more we wear this comfortable cozy footwear. Slippers, like all shoes go through fashion trends. They are mentioned in literature and fairy tales.

Sandals

The sandal is the simplest of footwear. It consists of a sole held to the foot with straps. It's made of various materials in different regions around the world. Worldwide, it is probably the oldest and most widely worn of all footwear.

Cinderella's Glass Slippers

This classic fairy tale has more than 500 versions. In each account, the slippers are made of gold, silver or some rare metal and sometimes covered in gems. In early French versions, Cinderella wore slippers of white squirrel fur, but this was changed from "vair" to "verre" meaning glass. In literature, shoes are a symbolic means through which women find grounding in the world and have their lives changed for better or worse. Shoes symbolize authority and power or humility and servitude depending on the context in which they are found. In many superstitions, shoes appear as good or bad luck omens. A great pair of shoes can seem magical and women tend to collect lots of them.

ANIMALS & BIRDS

What would our world be without these species? Their feeding relationship keeps nature in balance. From pest control to reproduction and pollination, they play a vital role in our lives. Animals and birds are our companions, workers, eyes and ears. Since caveman days, they have provided clothing, shelter and our food source. We have domesticated some, while others remain in the wild. No matter what, they are an important part of our lives and we need them.

Indian Ponies, 23" x 29." Assorted fabrics and yarns, feathers attached to the top left corner were hooked separately and layered. The edging is braided leather. Hung from a wooden arrow. 1st. Place, Calgary Stampede Arts and Crafts, 2009

The Indian tribes of Alberta are a big part of the Stampede. To include them I added feathers to the horse manes (and also I like feathers). The background is mostly yellow, to represent the grains and grasses of Alberta. All the strips used in the piece are hand cut with scissors and do vary in size for textural interest. I do not dye any fabric, instead choosing from my stash on hand, which often dictates the colours used. When doing animals, I always start with the eyes, as they can set the mood and character. I have tried to give life and character to every horse. I am often asked how long a piece like this takes to complete. This is determined by the difficulty of the subject, the amount of detail, the size of the strips and the hooking technique. Usually 3-5 minutes per square inch. Indian Ponies took about a month to complete, working at a fairly steady pace.

Wild Horses, 14"x16." Cotton fabrics & yarns.

Feathering the Nest, 16"x20." Assorted cottons and other fabrics and real feathers sewn on after hooking. If you look closely, you'll see a golden egg in the nest.

Blue Heron, 10"x22."
Mainly cotton fabrics.

Ripples, 7.3"x 9.8." Cotton fabric, with touches of white satin and real down feathers worked into the feather element.

Who Gives a Hoot? 15.5"x21." Cotton fabrics with trapunto under the bird. The background is reverse-hooked.

Snowy and Harem, 18"x24." Mostly cottons.

The Hare, 12"x18."
Mostly cotton fabric, the hare was hooked with yarn.

Eight Cats, 16" x 32"
Assorted fabrics and yarns.

Ying-Yang Fish, 22"x29." Cotton fabric. Center fish from Dover Chinese designs, the rest is Sharon's design.

Steller's Blue Jay, 13.5"x15." Cotton fabrics.

PEOPLE

Each individual that we encounter is an important part of our lives. Forming connections and relationships is a major part of our identity. It is from this web of people we get a sense of our personal worth and resilience. Our connection to others is a part of our most important life experiences. Each person and their stories really matter.

Lady with a Hat, 10.5"x26." Assorted cotton fabrics and yarn. The hat is chamois leather, trapunto on foam board. Uneven edge.

Knitting for The Troops, 15"x16." Assorted fabrics, yarns, ribbon, photo printed on fabric. Real knitting was attached in place, needles are screwers with bead ends. Quilt fabric border. Women across Canada helped with the war effort; knitting, wrapping bandages, making care packages from home and writing letters to the troops overseas. The photo is of Sharon's father in law from the First World War. Made for Women's Hands Building a Nation, a travelling exhibit celebrating Canada's 150th anniversary.

I have been a recycler for years, taking apart clothing and remaking it into new garments or things for the home. Using old magazines and catalogues to make collages and paper dolls, broken glass and stones to make mosiacs and anything else that catches my eye.

Oh What a Feeling, 24"x36." Assorted fabrics, mostly cotton. Matched set with Bad Hair Day (next page) for a woman's bathroom.

Bad Hair Day, 12.5"x16." Assorted fabrics, satin & yarns.

Stampede Romance, 16.5 "x 15.5." The heads were hooked separately and layered over the hooked background. The hats are clipped loops, and hair is yarn. The rest is hooked with cotton fabric, trapuntoed onto a foam board. *It's not only about two people, it's about Canada & USA working and getting together as they do at the Stampede.*

The series on the previous page was made for Sharon's local YWCA, along with Resilience (page 29) and Ripples (page 68). Notice Sharon's deft detail and shading in such small pieces.

1. Embrace the Child Within, 7.3"x9.8." Cotton and assorted fabrics, light trapunto on foam board.
Figure raised from background. Colourful child's chalk drawing on sidewalk as seen around the community. White picket fence with flowers and hint of red house and tree in background is down the street from me on 8th Ave. and fit in with the colourful happy scene I wanted to create. A little girl down the street was the inspiration for this piece. She is always drawing on the sidewalk and was showing me she had learned to play hop scotch.

2. Fishing with Grandpa, 7.3"x9.8." Cotton and assorted fabrics, light trapunto on foam board.
Boy and Grandfather teaching fishing, figures raised from background. Since all the other pieces have females in them, I chose males for this one.

3. Bridges, 7.3"x9.8." Cotton and assorted fabrics, light trapunto on foam board.
Person walking across bridge, figure raised from background. These old bridges are part of our past and yet important to the movement of people today. Fall scene, warm clothing, with red scarf a symbol of hope and brighter days. I wanted the person to be small in comparison to the structure surrounding.

4. Exercise is Good, 7.3"x9.8." Cotton and assorted fabrics, light trapunto on foam board.
Woman running on park pathway. Figure is raised from background.
Bow River and the Zoo in background with foliage in foreground to create distance. I see women running along the pathway almost every time I walk in the park.

(right) Shovels in the Ground, 11.5"x13."
Assorted fabrics and leather, trapunto and layering.

I like that working with fibre connects me with women who have made things for the home using techniques handed down from generation to generation.

They carry on traditions within the home of culture, food, needlework and often work with the young and the old.

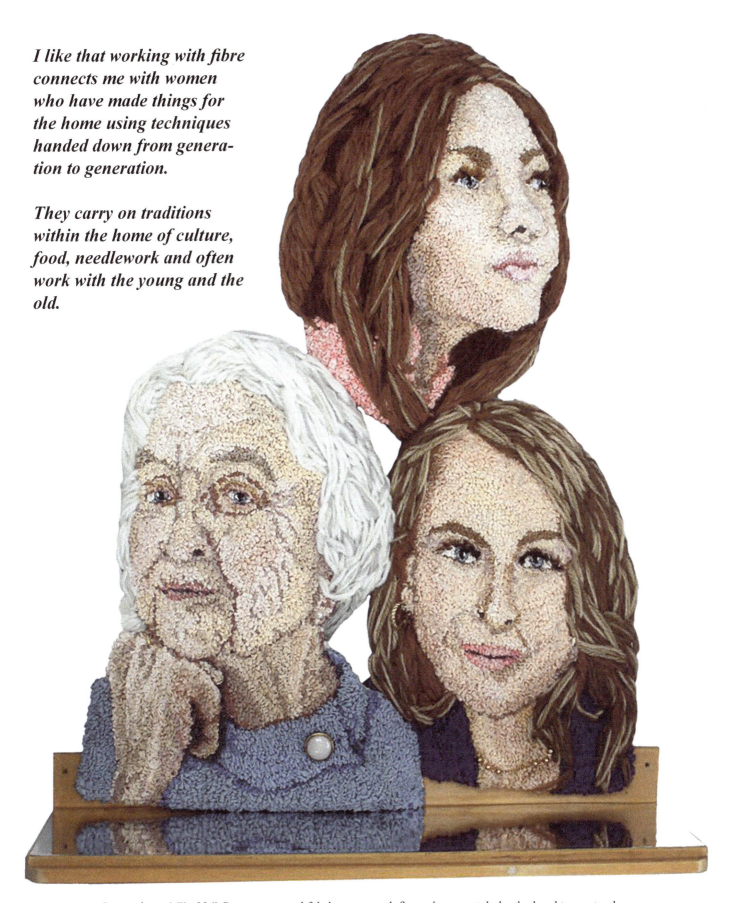

Generations, 16"x 22." Cotton, assorted fabric, yarn, each figure is separately hooked and trapuntoed

(opposite page) Freedom, 16"x21.5." Assorted cotton fabrics, like jean fabric etc. Trapunto under the figure and embroidered grass in foreground. *It represents being unfettered by society, enjoying the freedom to do what one feels like. Breaking out of the "box" we often find ourselves, developing as an individual.*

DAYS of CHILDHOOD

The moment I think of childhood, so many happy memories come flooding back to me. Mostly it is the nostalgia of not worrying, exploring, discovering and being in the moment. The early adventures of growing up... these are the times we most fondly remember.

New Calf, 21.5"x23.75." Polar fleece, misc. fabrics. Trapunto on a foam board.

Girl on a Tire Swing, 17"x23." Assorted cotton fabric, yarn. Uneven edge, wrapping (trees with yarn, tire with ribbon), layering, trapunto.

Relaxation, 14"x26." Cotton fabrics and trapunto.

Flowers For Mom, 17.5"x19." Assorted cotton fabrics. Uneven edge and trapunto under the girls.

Since fibre art is a relatively young form of art, there is more room to break away from traditional boundaries and create something entirely new.

Fresh Snow, 10"x18." Yarns. Uneven edge and trapunto. Snaps added for buttons and fur detail sewn on.

Kite Flying, 11.5"x19.75." Cotton fabrics and yarn. Uneven edge, embroidery, trapunto, layering.

Mudders, 16"x16.5." Assorted fabrics. Uneven edge, wrapping, embroidery and trapunto.

Treehouse, 18.5"x38.5" Assorted fabrics. Uneven edge, wrapping, the boys and steps are layered. Leaves sewn on after hooking. The grass base is trapunto.

PICTORIALS

I have always had an interest in history, which has so many fascinating stories, and from it, gives me ideas, be it of materials used, techniques or my own personal view of it.

Arabian Nights, 24"x38." A real assortment of fabrics and yarns as well as embelishments, sheer veils were sewn on the dancer's faces. *This was a commissioned piece. The couple used to read the 1001 stories to the kids. I suggested we limit it to 4 stories. They asked for camels, palm trees, and belly dancers. I designed the two main characters on the preferences of the clients. They wanted it to look like a rug with some meaningful symbols on border. They were thrilled with the results and wanted the pattern I had drawn for the grand kids to colour!*

Agriculture, 27.5"x36." Cotton fabrics. 1st Place in section, Calgary Stampede, 2010. Part of the traveling rug show, Tribute to the Prairie Elevator in Western Canada. Sharon's husband carved the wheat decorations on either side of the hanging with pine wood.

Up in the Haymow, 21"x22." Framed with old barn boards. Assorted fabrics and yarns. Used hooked and cut loops, different loop heights, embroidery & embellishments. The girl on rope was hooked separately and layered on the hooked area after a friend made the rope. You can see the layering of the girl on the rope side view (right).

Moscow Churches, 17"x18." Assorted fabrics, border shaped and trapuntoed on foam board. Uneven edge.

I want my art to be enjoyed, be it the story, the details, or a bit of whimsy. To create an emotional connection to the viewer.

Corvette, 20"x24." All kinds of fabrics, cotton, shiny, silver, satin. The metallic fabrics were tricky to hook, as was the receding floor.

Memorial Library Calgary, 24"x36." Assorted yarns, from an old post card and commissioned for the library's 100th birthday.

The technique is very simple, allowing much room for developing my ideas, yet slow enough in its execution to allow thinking things out as I work. The enjoyment of texture and colours of materials that I use to create art... the stories with this old craft are exciting.

Fibre art lets me take a piece of nature, a memory, a piece of history, a person, and turn it into a personal statement.

Native Women & the Fur Trade, 24"x36." Cottons, wool, yarns, leather, beads, trapunto, border faux fur. This collage represents contributions native women made to make the fur trade a success in Canada. Part of Womens Hands Building a Nation traveling show celebrating Canada's 150th anniversary.

North Wind, 12"x21.5." Assorted fabrics and yarn.

Snowflakes, 9"x17." Cotton, satin, velvet and yarn, designed from doodles.

Teacups, 8.5"x20.5." Cotton fabrics and purchased tassel.

Tea Time, 14.5"x44." Table runner, Assorted cottons a bit of silver fabric. Border meant to look like lace.

100

THE LADY & THE UNICORN

In 2020, I read a book about the Unicorn Tapestries. I thought it would be interesting to set them in a modern city, as we see unicorns today.

Sound, 16"x23.5." Yarns, assorted fabrics and embellishments.

Smell, 16"x23.5." Yarns, assorted fabrics and embellishments. All the pieces are hooked on rug warp and attached to a foam board with a canvas backing.

102

Sight, 16"x23.5." Yarns, assorted fabrics and embellishments.

Taste, 16"x23.5." Yarns, assorted fabrics and embellishments. Like the original Unicorn tapestries, now on display in the *Musée de Cluny* in Paris, the first five were devoted to the five senses, Hearing, Smell, Sight, Taste, Touch.

Touch, 16"x23.5." Yarns, assorted fabrics and embellishments. *Because of the tactile nature of fibre, it is a medium that practically begs to be touched as well as seen.*

Of My Own Free Will, 16"x23.5." Yarns, assorted fabrics and embellishments. The original title of the final French tapestry is *A Mon Seul Désir*. Historians debate its meaning, but some of the interpretations are 'by my will alone,' 'with my unique desire,' 'love desires only the beauty of the soul,' and 'love and understanding.'

ABSTRACTS & GEOMETRICS

Conceptual ideas are often not readily seen or experienced. It is about the balance and placement of lines, forms, shapes and colour. It is an observance of the world, but not achieved with reality. There is a uniqueness in these elements that are non-representational. You are free to explore and assign your own meaning to the work.

Mystic, 17.5"x23." Cotton fabrics. A series of woman symbols, the background is hooked mainly in swirls of blue, the color representing the Virgin Mary.

Chinese Foot Stool, 13"x19." Cotton fabrics, colors designed match a couple of antique chairs and pick up designs on a Chinese chest in Sharon's living room.

Simply Swirls, 19"x19." Pastel cottons. Top for a sewing stool. Design was inspired by shells.

Egyptian Motif, 25"x36." Assorted fabrics from sewing ends, designs from book of Egyptian motifs. Sharon's second attempt at rug hooking.

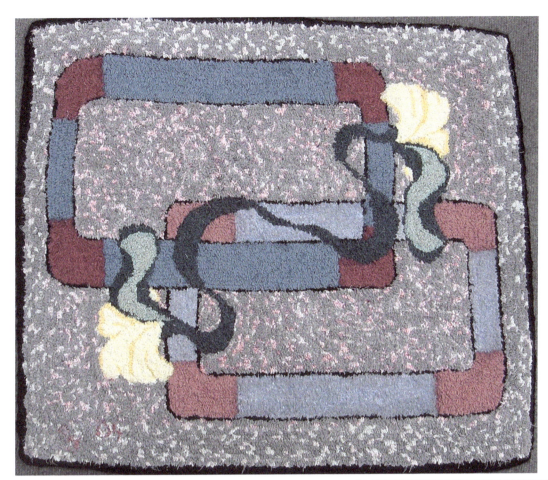

Yellow Flower Rug, 21"x26." Cotton fabrics background is an old patterned sheet.

Sharon's First Rug, 20"x24." Cut wool strips. Her first and only class almost turned her off hooking. I, for one, am very grateful she didn't quit!

111

Swirls, 10"x14." Chenille yarn and assorted other yarns on foam board, wrapping, uneven edge. *This one is mostly playing with colours and swirly shapes. Sometimes I do pieces like this just to try ideas and fill in time till I come up with a real piece to work on. It uses up bits and pieces.*

Chinook Wind Goddess, 8" diameter. Assorted fabrics and yarn. Symbolizes the wind from cold to warm, which is what happens in a "chinook" in Calgary.

Into the Light, 16"x57." Mostly cotton fabrics, with trapunto on foam board and wire. 8" fringe made from fabric. *I started thinking of the dark days of COVID-19 and how we would be progressing into brighter times. How small things can grow and become something new and beautiful. Each person who has seen this piece has had their own interpretation.*

Autumn is Messy, 10"x20.5." Assorted fabrics and yarns. Gold metallic yarn, machine stitched to canvas back. Just playing with ideas and materials.

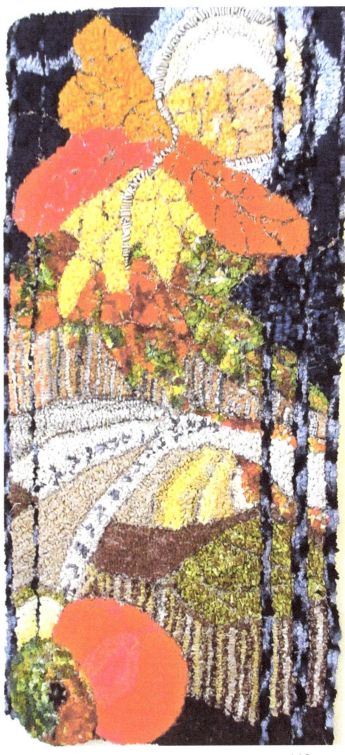

OF A COMMON THREAD

This magnificent collection represents the many cultures that have come together in Canada. It is available for sale, but only as a group.

Sharon wrote: Each piece represents a woman who came to this country originally from someplace else. Because cloth and clothing is a major part of women's culture, these pieces are made from cloth, yarns and thread. Much of the materials were recycled.

There are 27 pieces, each representing a country or region of origin, and the various major waves of immigration to Canada. Since people have come from so many different places, I had to narrow the number of pieces down, so chose the alphabet as my goal. I added one more for the USA, as many came there first on their way to Canada.

We have all come from somewhere else to settle this land from many diverse cultures, bringing something of that culture to pass on and to share. Each of us must adapt as did our ancestors to changing environments, yet preserve some of our roots. Culture is preserved through food, dress, music and the keeping of traditions. Women keep that cycle of life, culture and place in motion.

Women have found the time to create beauty in ordinary things. Skills that are often labour intensive were and are passed from one generation to the next. Fibre arts have always been considered women's work, usually done in the home and for domestic use. I have depicted these twenty-seven women's heads in cloth and yarns, using new and old techniques, hence, another common thread.

Inuit

East Coast Mic Maq

Metis

West Coast Haida

Plains Native

As you examine these portraits, keep in mind they average 12"x12," so every bit of detail and embellishment has been achieved within a relatively small space.

Great Britain

France

Scotland

116

Norway

Finland

Ukraine

Russia Balkans

Italy

Netherlands

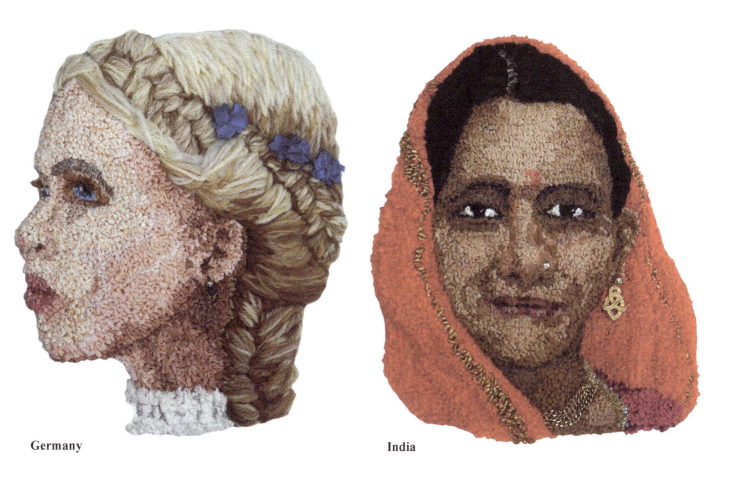

Germany

India

Philippines   **Middle East**

USA

121

CUSHIONS & BAGS

Cushions are small, portable works, fast to make and a way of testing ideas, using up strips from other projects. They are saleable, useful and make nice gifts.

Chicken Scratch, assorted fabrics and yarn.

Handsome Rooster, assorted fabrics.

Butterfly, assorted fabrics.

Bluebirds, assorted fabrics and yarns.

Tulip Garden, assorted fabrics.

Daffodil, assorted fabrics.

Sunflower, assorted fabrics.

Flanders Poppy, assorted fabrics.

Supreme Sultan Iris, assorted fabrics.

Rodeo Girl Iris, assorted fabrics.

Chasing Rainbows, assorted fabrics and yarns. Background was reverse-hooked. The yellow part of the beard was cut loops.

Yellow Iris, assorted fabrics.

Morning Glory, assorted fabrics.

Pansies, assorted fabrics.

Pink Flower Butterfly, assorted fabrics.

Red Poppy, assorted fabrics and yarns.

125

Firebird, assorted fabrics.

Tree of Life, assorted materials. The four birds represent Sharon and her husband, and their two children.

Autumn Sunset, assorted fabrics from a bag of warm colors.

Bamboo, assorted fabrics and yarn.

Buddy, assorted fabrics.

Cat Dreams, assorted fabrics.

Buck Deer, assorted fabrics and yarns.

Trout, assorted fabrics. A pair to the Buck Deer. The Johnstons' call this set the 'dinner pair.'

Three Graces, assorted fabrics and yarns.

Rabbit Seasons, assorted fabrics.

White Hunter, yarns and cottons.

Winter Scene, velvet, satin and yarns.

Green Swirls and Purple Flowers, assorted fabrics.

Chinook Headache, assorted fabrics.

Celtic Rainbow, assorted fabrics.

Art Deco, assorted fabrics.

Brown Sampler, assorted fabrics and yarns.

Blue Sampler, assorted fabrics and yarns.

Double-cross, assorted fabrics.

Fireworks, assorted fabrics and yarns.

Most of Sharon's bags were for laptops, as requested. She designs them with lots of special pockets to make them even more useful. They are very durable; she herself has carried the same craft bag to rug hooking events for 10 years, and it's still going strong.

Two Small Bags, 8"x8." Assorted fabrics and yarns.

Yellow and Black Laptop Bag, 13"x14." Only front hooked, geometric study in yellow.

Craft bag hooked front, back and sides, 15"x17." Assorted fabrics and yarn. Contains lots of pockets inside. Flower closure hooked separately. Wood handles.

LadyBug, 14"x12.5." Cotton fabrics. A study in greens. Designed as knitting bag for an elderly lady who loved Lady Bugs.

131

Horseshoes, 15"x18." Mostly cotton. The horseshoes are hooked with metallic fabric. Made for a fellow rug hooker.

Purple Circles, 15.5"x15.5." Assorted fabrics. Hooked pocket on back. Designed to carry laptop & files.

Rita's Craft Bag, 6"x21." Cotton fabrics. This was a commissioned piece made for the person who started the Tribute to Prairie Grain Elevators that toured Western Canada.

Seagrass, 15"x16." Cotton fabrics on a velvet base, wood handle, hooked back pocket. A study in greens.

Movements 13" x 15." Assorted fabrics. Laptop bag.

Movements, 13"x15.5." Assorted fabrics. Laptop bag.

Sunflowers, 14"x12." Cotton fabrics.

PROJECTS

Doors, 12"x12"x12.". Various yarns and fabrics. Each side has many doors, some with padlocks.

This is my latest piece called Doors. It is a covered wood box that my husband made for it. I made a female doll on one side opening a door, and a male doll on the top, trying to open the centre trap door! Pandora's box, maybe. What is behind the doors? Opportunities, secrets, traps, who knows what? Maybe the doors are just about the choices we make and the results of those.

This box is classic Johnston. To Sharon, no surface, flat or otherwise, need be unadorned with her whimsical art. It's a wonderful segue into our first practice project: Alphabet Blocks.

When making 3-D items I stuff them, use plastic containers, wire, or plastic mesh to make the shape. You need to experiment here to see what works best and remember to allow enough extra backing to sew together the piece. Sometimes you will use more than one piece to create the work.

Her dolls are sewn over a wire structure, with stones for heads, which she covers with nylon stocking to paint the faces. And don't forget to notice all the small details, like this tiny spiderweb. Later we'll get into how she makes those wrapped trees!

Project #1: Alphabet Blocks

Alphabet Blocks (5), 2"x2"x2." Designed and hooked by Judy Taylor.

Here's a dandy first try at hooking for that illusive third dimension. It's a group of 5 blocks, which contains every letter of the alphabet, plus a couple of extra "E's" and "A's." It will be a delightful toy for young ones just learning their letters, and a challenging game for older kids and grownups, seeing how many words they can form with these 5 blocks.

Don't kid yourself, I was able to make over 240 words with these 5, and only quit when my phone camera died! For more of a challenge, 'double the recipe' and make 10 blocks. You'll increase the possible words exponentially, including words of up to ten letters, plus you'll be able to use double consonents and vowels.

137

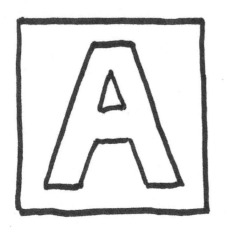
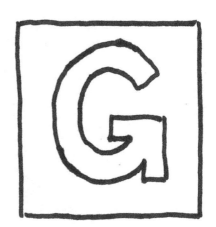

BLOCK # 1

These drawings are to scale to make cubes that are 2"x2" on each side. Copy these 5 pages and transfer the designs to the backing of your choice. Be sure to preserve the spacing between the squares, so you have enough to do your hem.

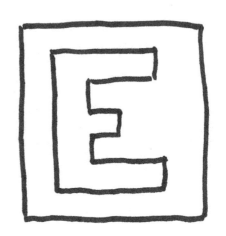

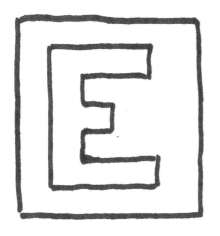

BLOCK # 2

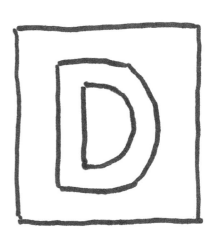

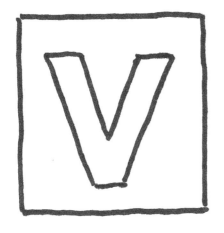
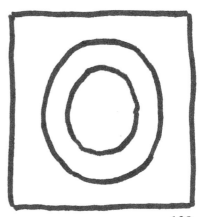

 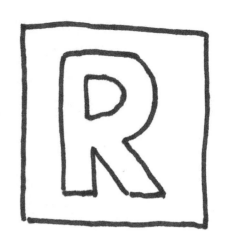

BLOCK # 3

BLOCK # 4

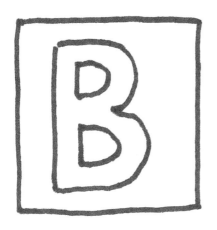
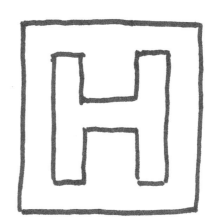

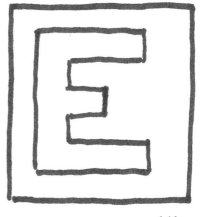

BLOCK # 5

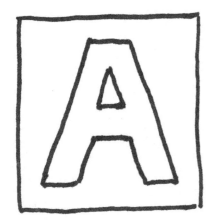
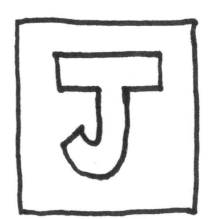

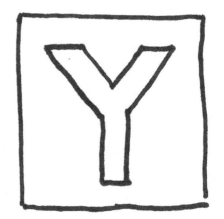

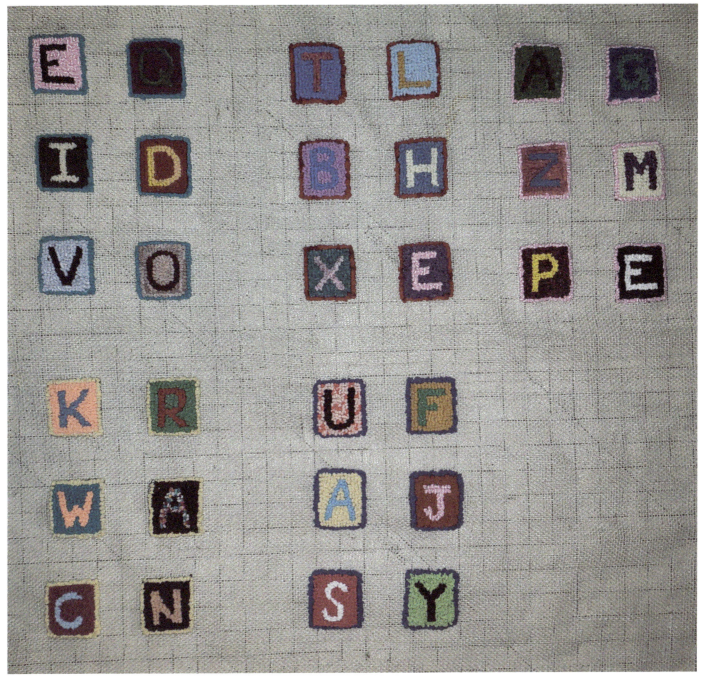

I hooked my squares with T-shirt strips in bright colors, but you do you. Here's what they looked like when the hooking was finished. You'll notice I chose the same outline color for each block.

 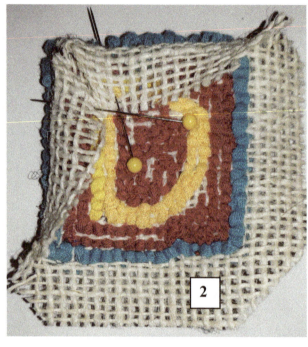

1. You will want to miter your corners to take out some of the bulk. First fold down the corner diagonally. Then fold down one side and pin it.

2. Fold down the other side and pin it. Hand sew down the diagonal fold line. Repeat steps one and two on the other corners.

3. Tack down the rest of the hem, bringing your needle up between the loops on the front, so all your stitches are covered by the loops. Then trim out the excess backing to reduce the bulk.

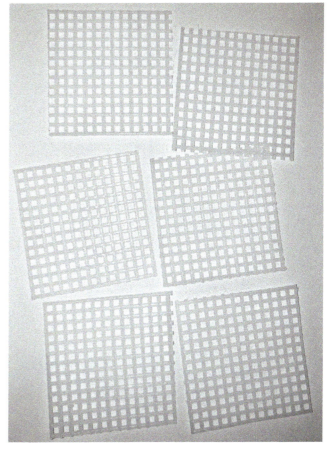

Hand sew your squares together, being careful to sew in between the loops so your stitches are hidden. Make sure you're sewing through the burlap, not just a loop. When you get to your sixth square, only sew down one side, like a hinged top.

Using the plastic mesh shown above, cut out six mesh squares. Since your hooked squares are 2"x2," you will want to cut your mesh squares slightly smaller so they will fit inside. Cut your mesh squares 1-7/8"x1-7/8." Make sure that you trim off any sharp extra bits, so your squares are smooth on the edges (otherwise they won't slip inside your hooked cubes).

Now you're going to lash your mesh squares together. Using embroidery thread, sew over your first tail. That way, you never have to tie knots.

When you run out of yarn, put your needle through a few previous stitches, then trim off the rest. No knots!

When your cube is all lashed together, slip it into your hooked cube.

Here you can see the mesh cube tucked inside the hooked cube. Now you can stitch that top square closed.

Finished!

147

Project #2: Ivy the Sheep

Ivy the Sheep, 15"x15." Designed and hooked by Judy Taylor.

Now, you can hook your sheep with anything you want, but since this book is called *Breaking the Boundaries*, I thought I'd show you how to hook with unspun locks of wool, for a wild, curly effect. You would never want to try this on a floor rug (how would you ever keep it clean?), but for a decorative object, why not?

For this project, I used a natural colored Lincoln fleece, which had patches of silver, gray, black and white. Not all breeds of sheep will work for hooking, but Border Leicester, Wensleydale and Mohair (the fiber of the Angora Goat) also work great.

You will need about 8 oz of washed wool for the project. Not "raw" wool, unless you know how to wash a wool fleece. It's not difficult, but if you don't know what you're doing, you can ruin it. You can Google the process, or just buy washed fleece.

Grasp a curly tip out of the bunch of washed wool, and peel it away. You might need to peel the lock apart again, until you get something thin enough to hook with. I generally aim for the thickness of a strand of yarn. It doesn't matter if they aren't all the same thickness.

(left) Lincoln Sheep from Sand Hill Farm in Ridgefield, WA. To order wool, contact eileenhordyk@gmail.com.

Here's another fun way to use washed locks of wool. The beard for this Santa was hooked with washed Border Leicester locks.

Victorian Santa, 18"x30."
Designed and hooked by Judy Taylor.

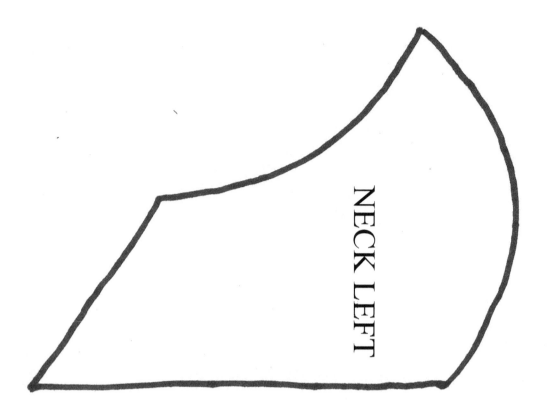

Hooked Pattern Pieces

Copy these first four pages to transfer onto burlap. Be sure to include the spacing between pattern pieces when you transfer them to the backing, so you'll have extra burlap to sew the pieces together.

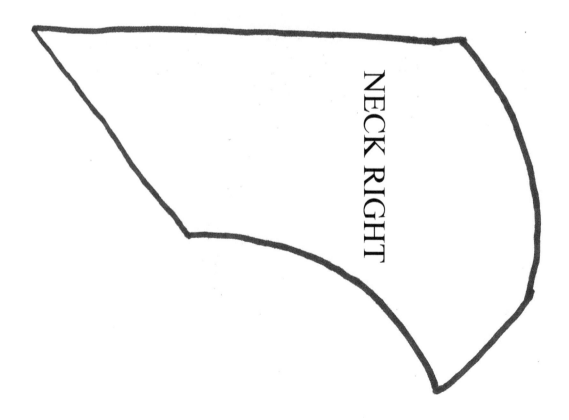

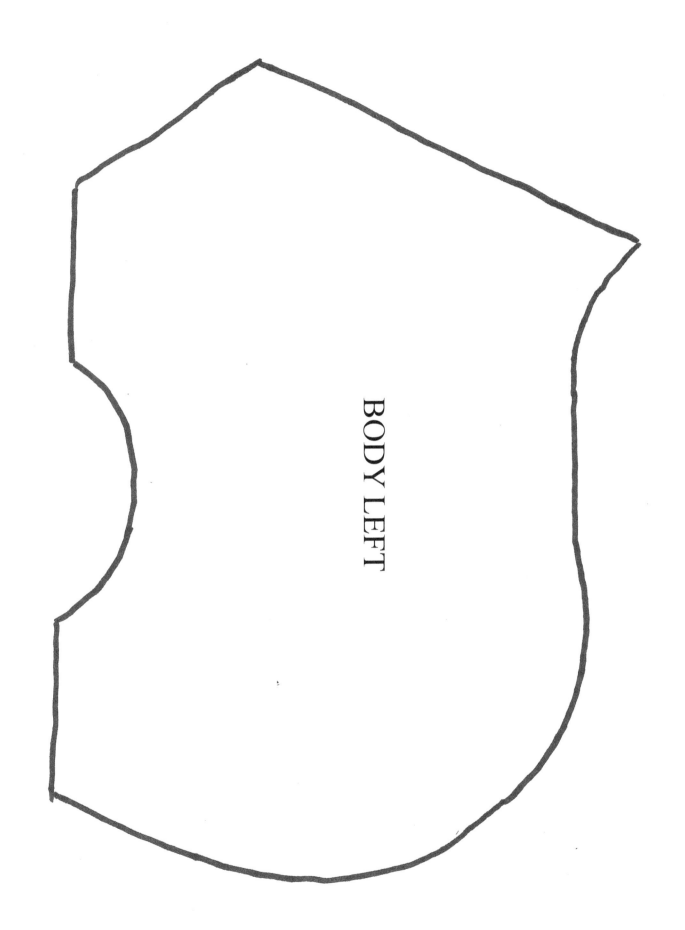

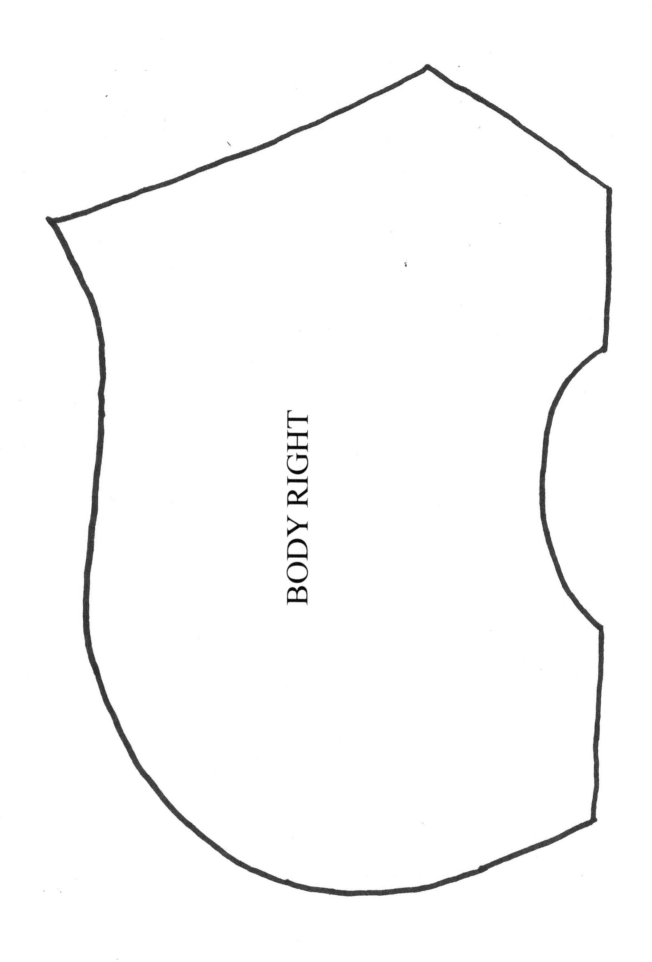

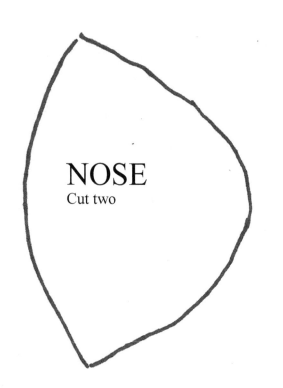

NOSE
Cut two

These are your fabric pieces to cut out. I used hand-dyed felted wool fabric, so the edges wouldn't fray, but you can work with any fabric you like.

Copy this page so you can cut out the pattern pieces.

EAR
Cut two

TAIL
Cut one

LEG
Cut eight

FOOT
Cut four

When hooking with a lock of wool, start with the curly end. Leave a tail about 1/2" or so. Then pull up your first loop. Once you've done the first loop, you can reach underneath and give the lock a couple of twists. Just enough to allow you to grab it easily with your hook. Bring up your loops about twice as high as you would with yarn or wool strips, to emphasize the curly look. You will probably get only 4-6 loops per lock. Then pull up your final tail and leave it there for now. Stagger your loops so you have those curly tails everywhere.

You will end up with something that looks like a lamb's skin, only in our case, the ewe that produced the wool is still alive and chewing her cud, which is nice.

You will notice that the curl is pretty well defined in the beginning (the outside of the fleece), and the lock tends to frizz more toward the other end (the inside or cut side of the fleece). That's fine, you'll trim some of that frizz away when you're done hooking.

Here you can see what the Body Right Side piece looks like hooked. The tails need some trimming, but don't trim them all away. Concentrate on trimming just the frizzy stuff, and leave the curly tails.

Here is the same piece after I trimmed away most of the frizz.

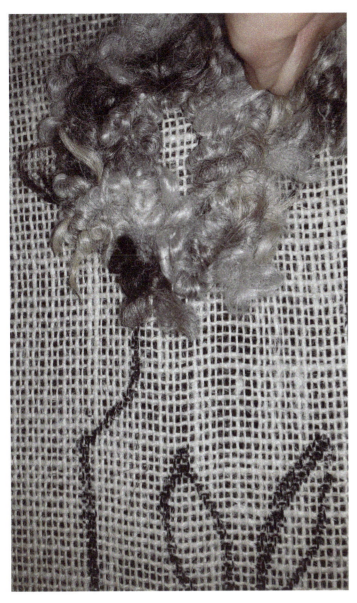

On the Tummy piece, don't hook inside the four darts. Those are there to shape the tummy later.

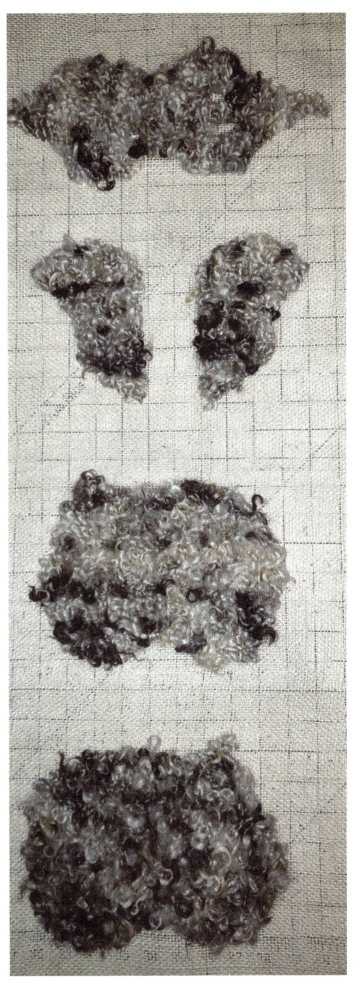

On the right, you can see all the hooked pieces finished.

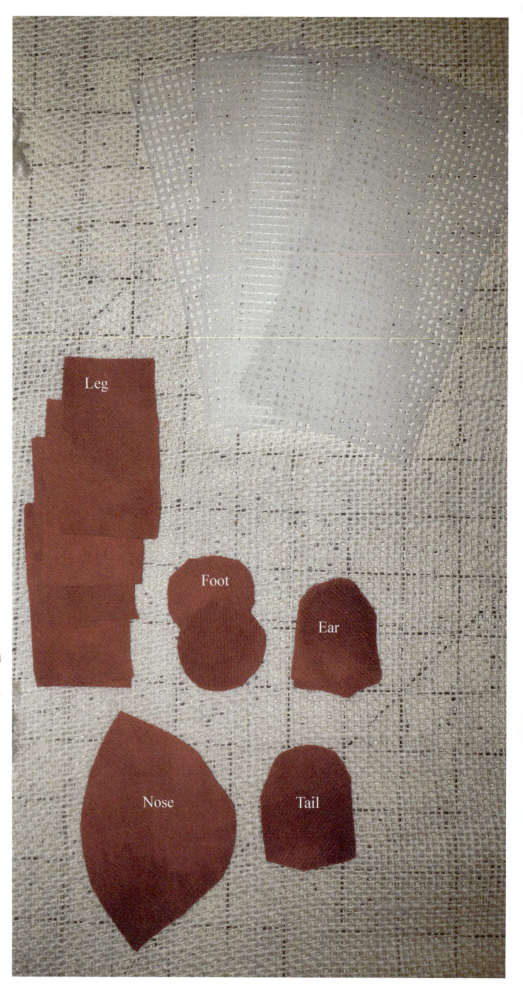

Here you can see I've cut out all my fabric pieces:

8 Leg pieces
4 Foot pieces
2 Ear pieces
1 Tail piece
2 Nose pieces

Using the same plastic mesh we used for the alphabet blocks, cut 4 pieces, each 6-1/4"x3-3/8." Trim off the sharp bits so you have smooth edges. We will be using the mesh to strengthen the legs so the sheep will stand.

Most of the sewing for Ivy the Sheep will be done by hand, like the Alphabet Blocks. I did use my sewing machine for some of the fabric parts. Since they are small pieces, I've found it easier to sew seams on the outside (so they show) rather than turning them inside-out (I can never press out a smooth seam because the pieces are so small).

On the left, you see I'm sewing the two nose pieces together, using a straight stitch.

Then I sew over the same area, this time using a zig-zag buttonhole stitch. That way, I preserve the edges of the fabric so they don't fray.

Here are the settings on my machine for the zig-zag buttonhole stitch. It's basically a very tight zig-zag.

If you don't have a sewing machine, you could certainly hand-sew all the fabric pieces, but the machine comes in handy if you do have one.

(And yes, that's a fortune cookie taped to my machine. "You will make a name for yourself in the field of fashion." How about that?)

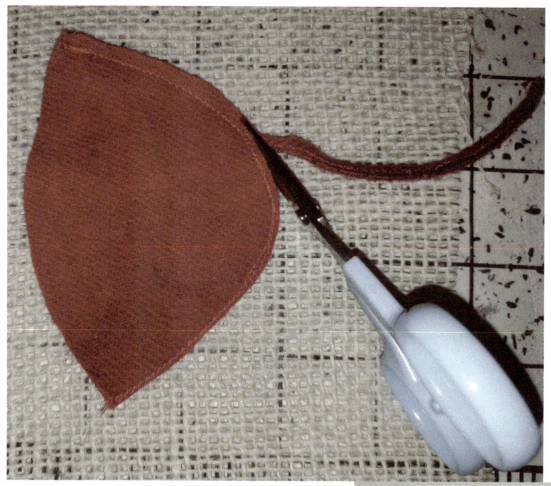

Above you can see that I trim off the extra selvedge, very close to the zig-zag line.

Next, fold the ear piece in half and sew it to one side of the face. Repeat this step on the other side of the face.

Here comes the fun part.

Pin the two neck pieces together, folding the burlap selvedge in.

You can see that, wherever possible, I like to have about 1" of burlap outside the hooked area. Most of it is going to be pushed inside. I don't trim too close to the hooked edge, because I'll be doing a lot of manipulating those pieces. I don't want the burlap selvedge to fall apart.

Just like with the Alphabet Blocks, you are going to hide your stitches in between the curly loops. Do make sure you are sewing through the burlap, not just a loop.

I like to do a row of stitching going one way, then take out the pins and stitch my way back to the starting point, for good measure.

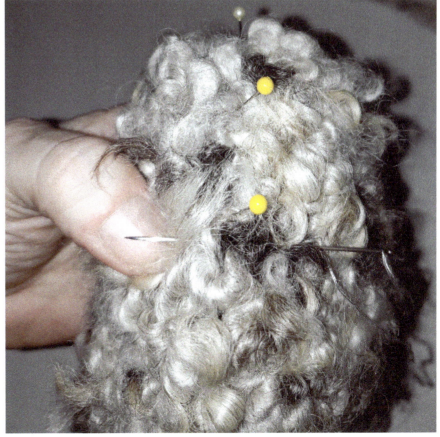

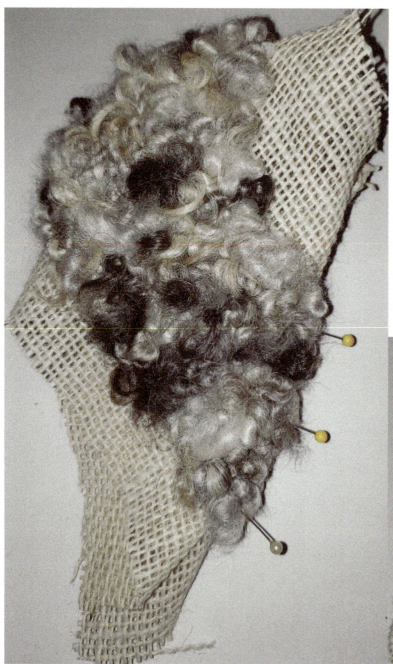

Here you see the top side of the neck piece is sewn; now I've pinned the front side of the neck closed.

I hand-stitch along that line, back and forth.

Next I tuck the extra burlap in the front of the neck to make ready to add the face.

I pin the face into the neck piece, lining up the top seams of the face and neck, as well as the bottom seams. This can take some adjusting to fit everything together.

Here I'm stitching all around the face, making sure I'm digging deep, sewing through the burlap and red fabric, not a loop of wool.

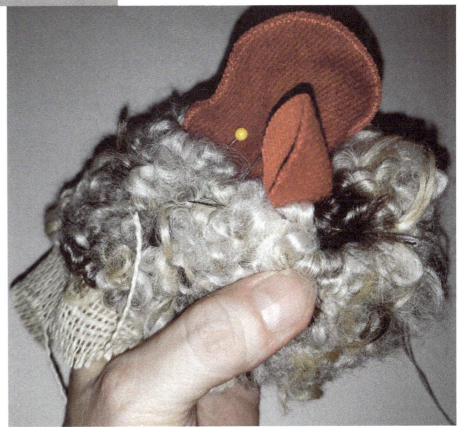

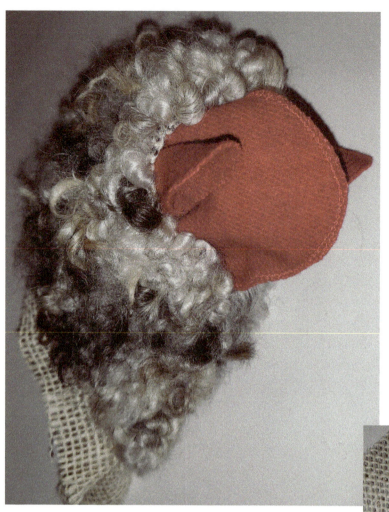

Hey, you made a face!

With the Tummy piece, you're going to need to notch the corners where the tummy turns into the top of the leg. (You might think of these as armpits)

Here you can see I've notched those two corners quite close to the hooked area.

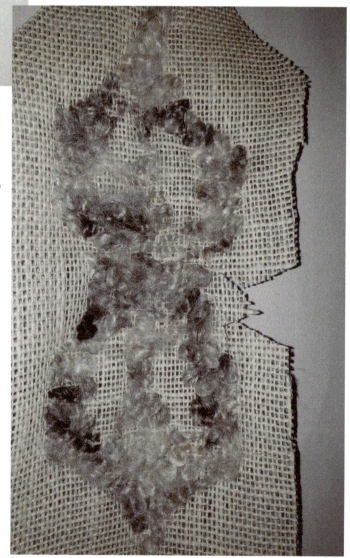

Then I reinforce that notch, to support the burlap in the Tummy piece.

You can see I've already reinforced the other notch (on the right) and I'm stitching the one on the left.

Notch the other side of the Tummy in the same way and reinforce the burlap.

Here I'm sewing those four darts closed on the Tummy piece.

And here's the Tummy piece with the notches reinforced and the darts sewn.

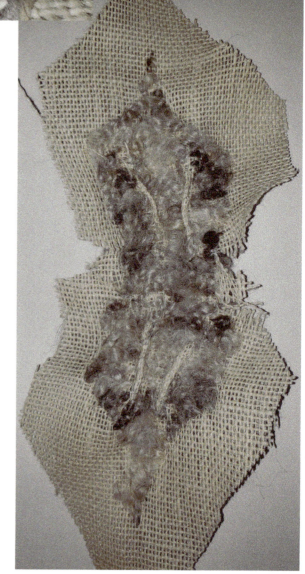

You'll need to reinforce the armpits on the two Body Side pieces as well, in the same way you did the Tummy.

Fold the Tail piece in half and hand-sew it to one side of the Body.

Above you can see that I do cut a notch in the back of the Body Side piece, just where the back curves into the neck. However, I don't cut the notch right down to the hooked edge, so no need to reinforce that. Do the same on the other Body Side piece. Then pin the two Body Side pieces together, just along the back. You aren't going to sew the whole back closed, though. Sew about one inch (on the left) then leave a gap, then sew the rump around the Tail piece. The gap in between is where you will be stuffing the sheep.

Above you can see that I have pinned the Neck to the Body, pulling the Body pieces together at the base of the Neck (the rest of the Body pieces should splay outwards from that point).

Then I stitch all around the neck.

Now we're going to start sewing the Tummy piece to the Body.

I start by pinning one side of the 'point' of the Tummy along the Body piece under the Tail.

Then I pin the other side of the 'point' of the Tummy piece to the other Body piece.

Notice that I have lined up the leg parts as well on the bottom.

Taking nice deep stitches, I sew the Tummy piece to the Body pieces.

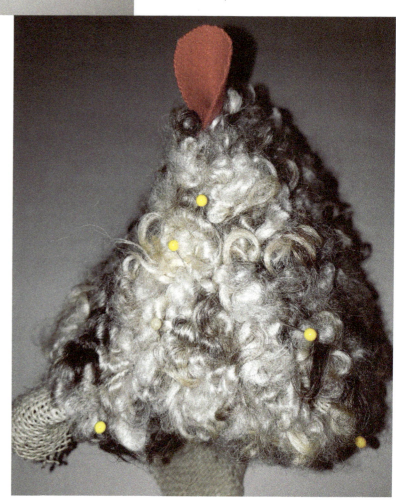

Above you can see I've pinned the other Tummy point into the front of the Body. If you have more of the point than you need, just tuck the extra inside and stitch everything closed. Remember to line up the leg parts, too. Below you can see I've pinned the Tummy side to the Body side, lining up the leg holes. Stitch.

Here you can see the Tummy is sewn to the Body. I tuck the extra burlap inside the leg holes.

This is a good time to stuff the face and neck. I use polyester stuffing for this, but you could use some of the leftover fleece, cut up felted sweaters, whatever you like.

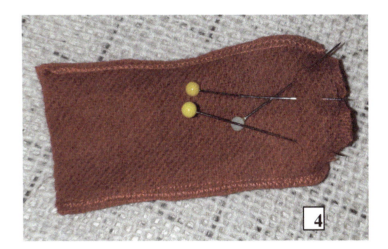
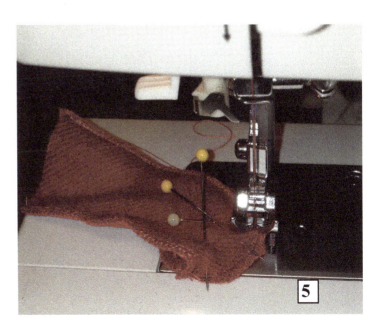

1. Sew the legs with a straight stitch.
2. Sew over the seams with a zig-zag stitch
3. Trim away the extra selvedge
4. Pin one side of the leg to half of the foot, then sew with a straight stitch
5. Pin and sew the other side of the foot with a straight stitch. It's much easier to sew one side of the foot at time.

Now you can zig-zag the foot over the straight stitch.

Then trim away the extra selvedge. Repeat these steps for the other three legs.

The four legs are done.

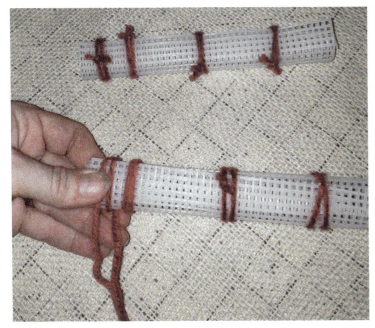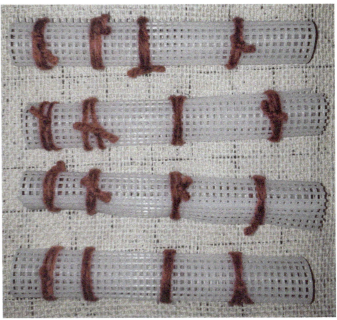

Roll up the plastic mesh so it will fit inside the legs. I wrapped the mesh up with yarn.

Here's what the four mesh sections look like rolled up. By tying them with yarn instead of sewing, it's easy to adjust them to fit inside the legs.

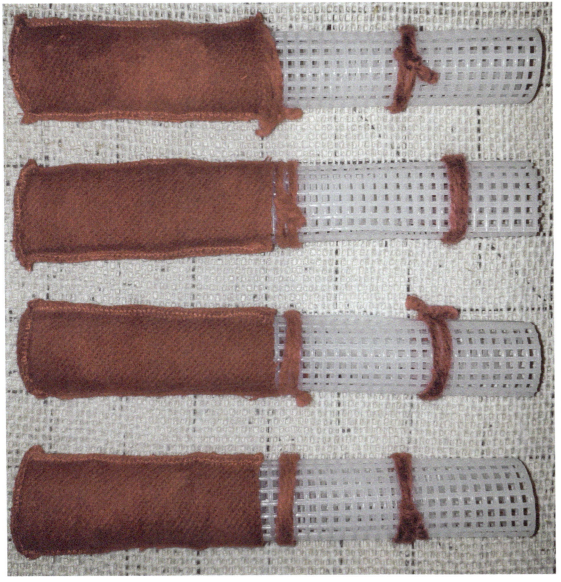

Why does the mesh stick up so far? That's the structure that allows Ivy to stand on her own.

177

Push the leg pieces into the leg holes, using scissors or a butter knife to tuck all the red material inside the hole. Don't pin or sew the legs just yet.

Stand Ivy up and adjust the placement of the legs, if necessary. Then you can go ahead and stuff the rest of the body, making sure you surround the mesh pieces.

When you're satisfied that the mesh parts are surrounded with stuffing, and she stands straight on all four legs, you can sew the legs to the body.

Then you can sew the back seam closed.

1. Cut out around 18 ivy leaves. I used hand-dyed wool fabric.
2. Sew a little dart in the bottom of the leaf
3. Shows what the leaf looks like with the dart sewn
4. Sew the leaves to a long piece of yarn. Wrap the leaf garland around Ivy's neck twice, tacking the yarn together to make a loopy vine.

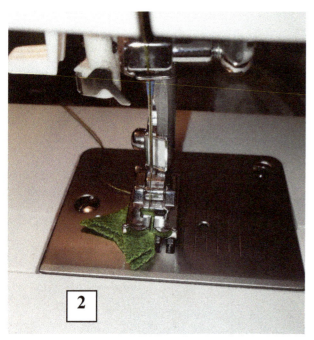

Mairzy doats and dozy doats and liddle lamzy divey

A kiddley divey too, wouldn't you?*

*If you remember that song, you're as old as me!

Project #3: Mischief

In Sharon's project, Carousel of Time, she hooked the horse, and the upper and lower sections of the carousel, then reverse hooked the background behind the horse. In the close-up above, you can see she also embroidered daisy-chains. All of this serves to create a subtle 3-D effect.

Carousel of Time, 18"x22."
Assorted fabrics and yarns.
Reverse hooking.

Mischief, 9"x14." Yarn for the dog and the shoes, T-shirt strips for the reverse-hooked background. Designed and hooked by Judy Taylor.

Mischief is an easy project to try reverse hooking for that subtle raised effect. I hooked the dog and shoes first with yarn, then flipped the project over and hooked the rug background with T-shirts. On the next two pages, copy the dog and shoes and transfer them onto the backing of your choice. I went with linen, because the weave is tighter.

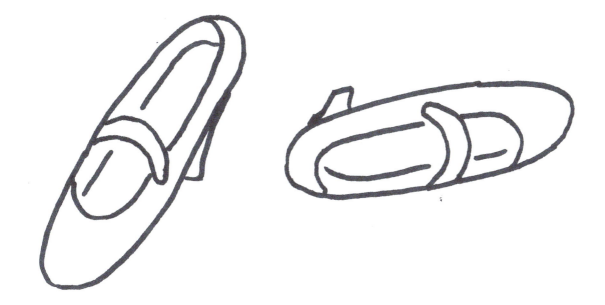

After transferring the dog and shoes, I drew a 9"x14" parallelogram. You can do the same, or an oval, or whatever you like for the background.

I marked the outline with straight pins, so I could draw it on the reverse side as well.

If you have a punch needle, you wouldn't have to copy the outline to the back, you can just hook the dog and shoes, and punch the background, but I hooked both sides, so I needed the outline on the back.

Following the straight pins, I drew the outline on the back.

The reverse hooking in the back left some space behind the dog and shoes. To preserve the raised effect in front, I wanted to support the dog and shoes so they wouldn't sink back.

Using the same template I used to transfer the dog and shoes, I cut out two layers of cotton quilt batting to support the areas in back. Depending on the height of your reverse hooking loops, you may need to adjust the thickness.

I tacked the batting behind the dog and shoes, bringing my needle up in between the loops so my stitches wouldn't be seen from the top.

Here you can see the batting tacked down.

I trimmed away the excess linen to do the hem. I trimmed off the corners for mitering, to reduce bulk on the corners.

I folded down the diagonal edge first, then pinned down one side of the mitered corner.

Here you can see I've pinned down the other side of the mitered corner, as we did on the Alphabet Blocks.

Pin down the rest of the hem all around. I sewed the diagonal miters first, then tacked down the rest of the hem, bringing my needle up in between the loops for hidden stitches.

The hem is tricky with reverse hooking, because you can't sew the hem to the loops; you have to bring your needle all the way through to the top.

Sharon uses this lightweight foam board to back her pieces. It's sturdy for something so light, and yet it's easy to cut and sew through.

Cut a parallelogram slightly smaller than the hooked piece.

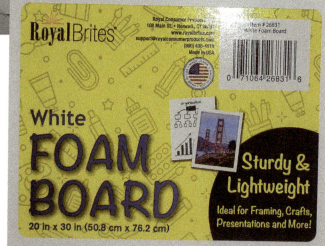

190

Stitch around the dog and shoes, bringing your needle up through the foam board to the top, hiding your stitches between loops.

By quilting around the main features, they will stand out from the reverse hooked background.

Here you can see the quilting stitches around the dog and shoes. This helps to make them stand out in front.

Sharon backs her pieces with matching T-shirt material. As soon as I learned that, I thought, "Of course! What a great idea!" T-shirt material stretches where you need it to, and lies flat where you need it to. This becomes even more important for projects with uneven edges, like the Trapunto Sunflower in the next section. Here you can see I pulled the backing material up in front, to cover that little bit of linen that showed after the hem.

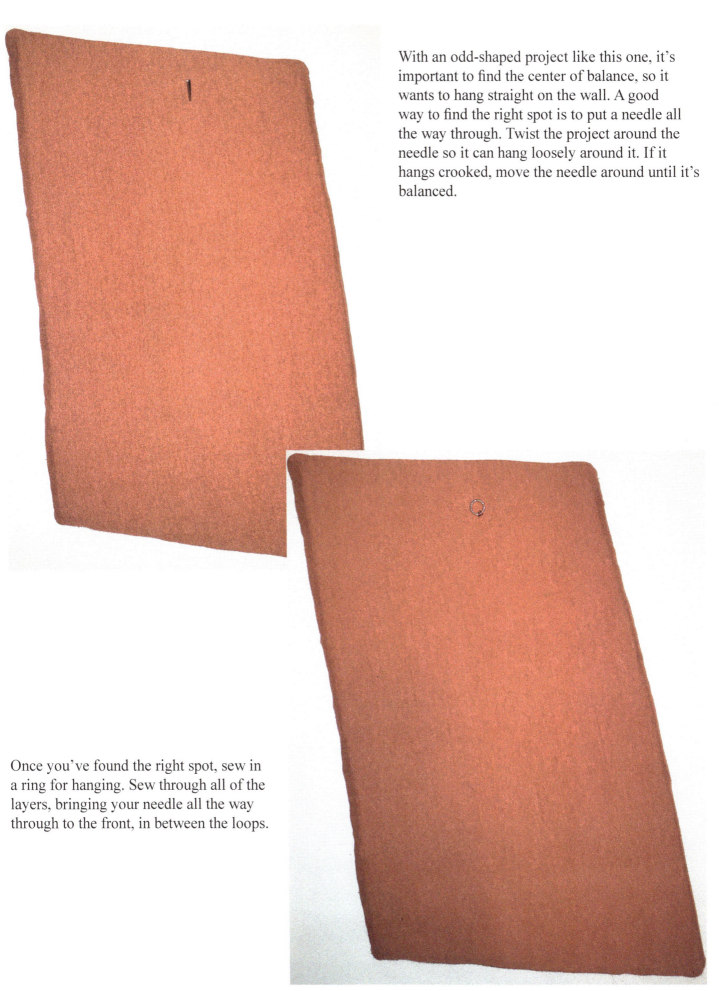

With an odd-shaped project like this one, it's important to find the center of balance, so it wants to hang straight on the wall. A good way to find the right spot is to put a needle all the way through. Twist the project around the needle so it can hang loosely around it. If it hangs crooked, move the needle around until it's balanced.

Once you've found the right spot, sew in a ring for hanging. Sew through all of the layers, bringing your needle all the way through to the front, in between the loops.

Final touch: I sewed yarn fringe to the rug.

On the side view, you can see the dog and shoes rise up.

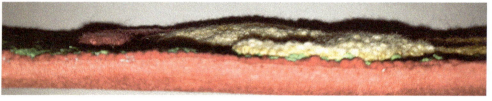

194

While we were working on this book, I wanted to make this hooked piece out of T-shirts. It's from a photograph of my mom on her wedding day, 1950, getting ready for her honeymoon.

Inspired by Sharon's work, I thought I would experiment with her uneven edges and make the piece follow the shape of the mirror and the figure in front, instead of the original square photo.

I showed it to Sharon, and she suggested I try doing trapunto on the figure outside the window.

It was surprisingly easy, and the end result was that when you see the piece in person, you really do get the effect of someone standing in front of a flat mirror.

Her Past and Her Future, 16"x18." Designed and hooked by Judy Taylor.

Below you can see what it looked on the side view. It's hard to see the quilting on a 2-D photograph! Now you will get a chance to try both Sharon's uneven edges and trapunto with Trapunto Sunflower.

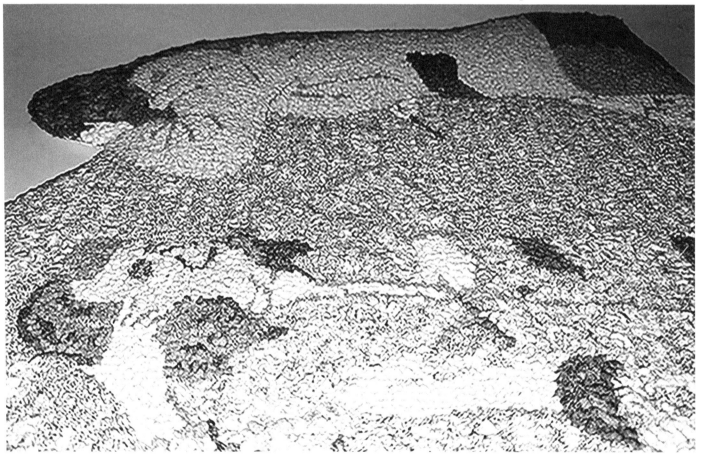

195

Project #4: Trapunto Sunflower

I hooked my Sunflower with T-shirt strips, but you can use any material you like. Maybe experiment with some of Sharon's suggestions: cotton, silk, satin, novelty yarns, etc.

Trapunto Sunflower, 9"x9.5." T-shirt strips and trapunto.
Designed and hooked by Judy Taylor.

Below you can see the side view.

Copy the two sides and tape them together to transfer the design to the backing.

It's not a bad idea to do a straight stitch on your sewing machine right next to the outline after you've drawn your design on the backing. You are going to be applying a light layer of glue on the edges before you cut the hooked pattern out, but it doesn't hurt to add a little extra support to the linen backing.

I always do this on my floor rugs, to prevent the linen from spreading out near the hooked edge.

Here you see the hooking is complete, so I am painting a light layer of Elmer's glue all around the hooked piece.

When the glue dries, you can begin to trim away the extra backing. This step can be nerve-wracking if you've never done it before, so go slow, take your time.

You will also need to notch those inside corners around the gold petals.

Just as we did with Ivy the Sheep, it's good to put in a few reinforcing stitches in that notch (right).

Here you can see I have pushed down the extra backing to make the hem. It's a little stiff, with the glue reinforcement.

Once I've folded the selvedge down, I trim away everything I don't need, and then tack down the hem. As always, it's important to make sure you are putting your needle all the way through to the linen backing, not a loop.

Here you can see the hem completed all the way around.

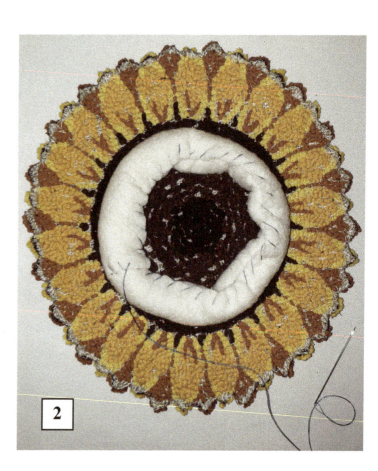

1. I made a 15" roll of cotton quilt batting
2. Then tacked the 'donut' to the center of the flower
3. I next made a 'sandwich' of batting, with a total of 5 layers, so I would have a little less padding in the middle of the flower.
4. Sandwich put together
5. Sandwich attached to the donut.

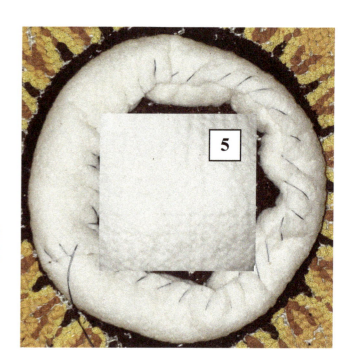

Next I cut out another piece of quilt batting to the size of the hooked piece.

Pulling the dark center of the flower around the donut, I tacked it down to the quilt batting. Remember to hide your stitches in between the loops on the top.

This is what it looked like from the top, with the center of the flower stitched to the quilt batting around the donut.

Notice that there is a little 'play' now on the petals, almost like a little ruffle. We're going to use that in a minute.

But first, I wanted the center of the flower to be slightly indented, so I tacked it down to the sandwich, through the quilt batting in back.

Then I notched the quilt batting, surrounding all of the yellow petals.

Here you can see that I am tacking down the corners of the batting, so most of it comes under the yellow petals, not the gold.

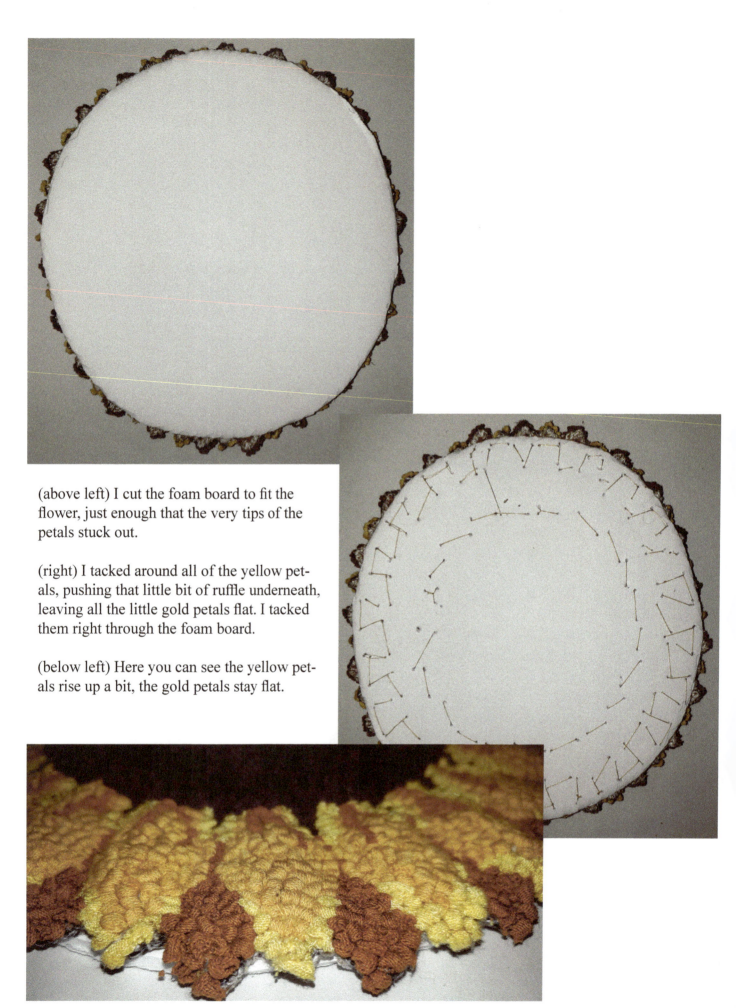

(above left) I cut the foam board to fit the flower, just enough that the very tips of the petals stuck out.

(right) I tacked around all of the yellow petals, pushing that little bit of ruffle underneath, leaving all the little gold petals flat. I tacked them right through the foam board.

(below left) Here you can see the yellow petals rise up a bit, the gold petals stay flat.

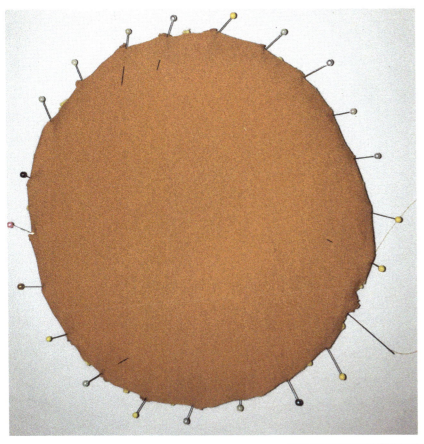

Since I hooked my Trapunto Sunflower with T-shirt strips, I chose the same gold material to cover the back. I sewed the T-shirt material to the flower, covering up the foam board.

(above) Here you can see what the hem looked like. The T-shirt material makes sewing the points very easy, stretching where I need it to.

(left) Attach a ring to the back for hanging. Bring your needle all the way through to the front, again hiding your stitches between the loops.

Hidden, 9"x13." Assorted cottons, uneven edge, trapunto, layering and wrapping of vines.

A little bit more about trapunto:

Notice how Sharon used trapunto in the face. She shaped the nose and cheek, then she padded the whole face so it looks like it's pushing out from the foliage.

You can also see her technique of layering in the pink flower and some of the leaves. You will get to try layering and wrapping in the next project, Hobbit House.

(above) Here's a great view of the trapunto effect on the face. The nose and cheek were shaped first, then the rest of the face was padded and stitched down. The eyelashes were hooked with (what else?) eyelash yarn!

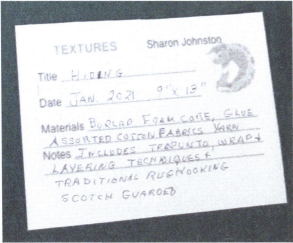

(above) Sharon prints her fabric labels, then writes the identifying information. She sews these to the backs of all her projects.

So now we've covered how to create 3-D projects with a rigid structure, and a padded structure. We've tried reverse hooking, trapunto and also, working with uneven edges on the Trapunto Sunflower.

Now we're going to put it all together, including her layering technique--and that magnificent wrapping of trees--in our next project, the Hobbit House.

209

Tasty Apples 12.5"x23." Sharon knitted the sweater and stitched it in place. The girl, apple and grass is trapunto, and Sharon embroidered some of the grass.

Night Sky, 18"x19.5." Assorted fabric, yarn wrap, trapunto, layered person, beads.

Another wonderful example of the wrapping of trees, an uneven edge, layering and trapunto.

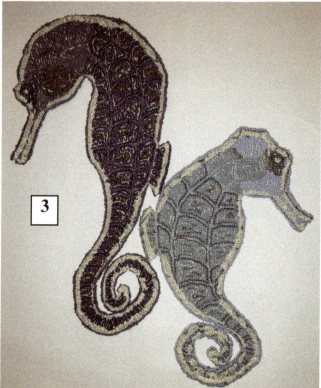
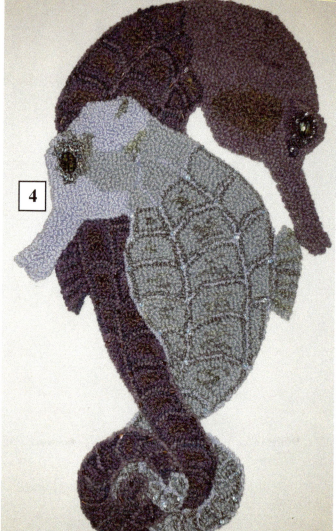

My first attempt at layering. I could have started with something easier, but as my mom likes to say, "Anything worth doing is worth doing to excess."

1. First I drew the two seahorses already entwined, then made a template for each, and hooked them separately.
2. I painted glue along the edges.
3. I tacked down the hem.
4. I (with trepidation!) wrapped them up together. Then I sewed bead eyes and bead decorations.

I drew out the shape on the foam board.

I could have used trapunto to lift up the higher layers, but instead, I built up extra foam board in the two places where the blue seahorse stuck out from the purple one.

Here's what the entwined tails looked like from the side. No need for trapunto here, the hooked pieces provided the shape. You can also see the hem, where I attached T-shirt material to the back, as I did for Mischief and the Trapunto Sunflower.

Seahorses, 13"x22." Yarn, beads and layering. Designed and hooked by Judy Taylor.

When my husband and I were married, we didn't have a bride & groom on our cake, we had glass seahorses, so I made this for our anniversary.

I use lots of wrapped cord in my work. A similar wrap technique as is used for the finished edge of rugs. You can wrap cord or rope of different sizes.

Also, you do not need to have the entire wrapped cord attached to the backing, letting you cross tree branches or let them hang as in the Fairy Tree piece. Pipe cleaners are handy for this, allowing you to shape the loose branches. You can use cloth, T-shirts and ribbon as well for wrapping.

Fairy Tree, 11.5"x15." Yarn, assorted fabrics. She attached wool leaves at end of pipe cleaners. Then wrapped the length, and tucked the pipe cleaners into the cord as she continued to wrap. The fairy was made and added last.

215

Project #5: Hobbit House

Hobbit House, 10.5"x6.5." Yarn, button for doorknob. Uneven edge, wrapping, trapunto and layering. Designed and hooked by Judy Taylor.

To make the Hobbit House, we'll be incorporating four of Sharon's signature techniques; uneven edges, trapunto, wrapped trees and layering.

For the other projects in this book, you could use the pattern pieces as shown, but with Hobbit House, you might enjoy enlarging the pattern, because once you start wrapping that tree, if you're like me, you will want to keep going!

Looking down from above, you can see the wrapped tree, the layered door and the trapunto grassy area.

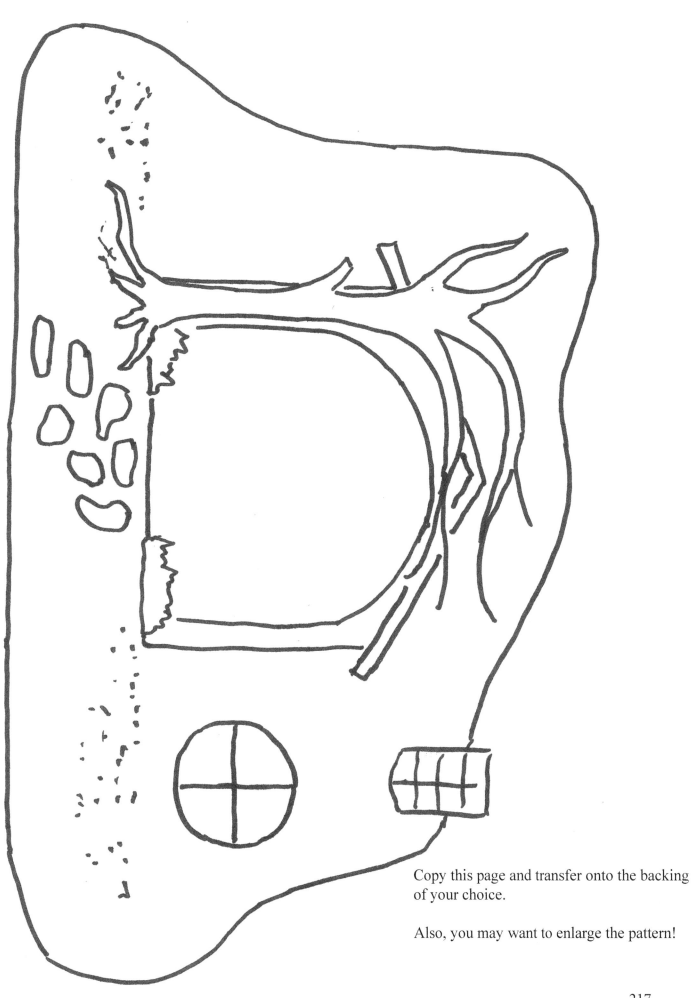

Copy this page and transfer onto the backing of your choice.

Also, you may want to enlarge the pattern!

217

Copy the door and transfer it onto the backing. Leave at least 1" of space around it so you have enough to hem the door.

Leave the little circle for the doorknob unhooked. You'll be adding a button later.

If you are enlarging the pattern, do the same with the door.

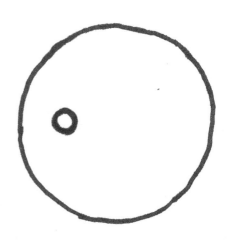

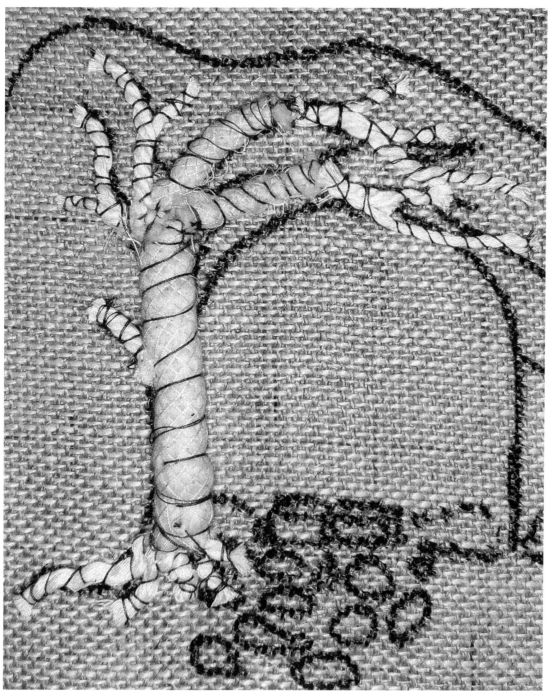

Here you can see I have sewn down various widths of cording to the linen.

I found this process addicting and fun. As you can see from Sharon's work, you can use this technique on any type of design; realistic, as in the Seasons series (pp. 14-17), whimsical as in the Fairy Tree (page 215), or abstract, as in Swirls (page 112).

(above left) Yarn for wrapping, embroidery needle and a tooth floss threader to aid in threading the needle (above right).
(below) I like to start my wrapping from the top with my needle, leaving a 1" tail that I will sew over as I begin the wrap.

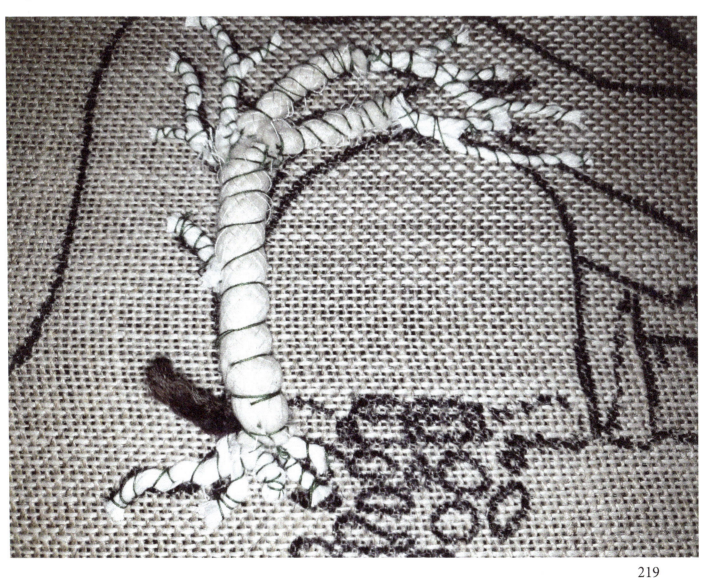

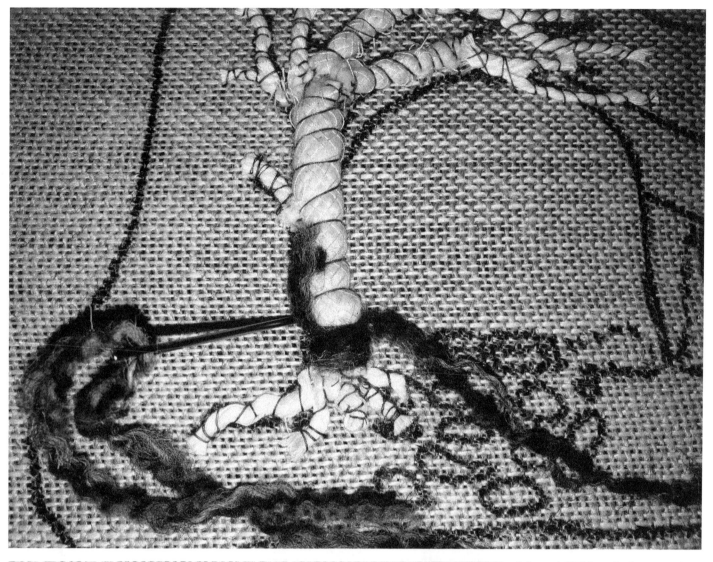

(above) Whip stitch around the cord, through the linen backing, while sewing over the beginning tail.

(left) When you run out of yarn, turn the work over and run your needle under some of the previous stitches. That way, you don't need to tie a knot.

The finished wrapping of the tree. I didn't do her 'cross-over' idea to overlap the branches with pipe cleaners instead of cording, because my sample project was so small, but it would work great if you decide to enlarge the pattern.

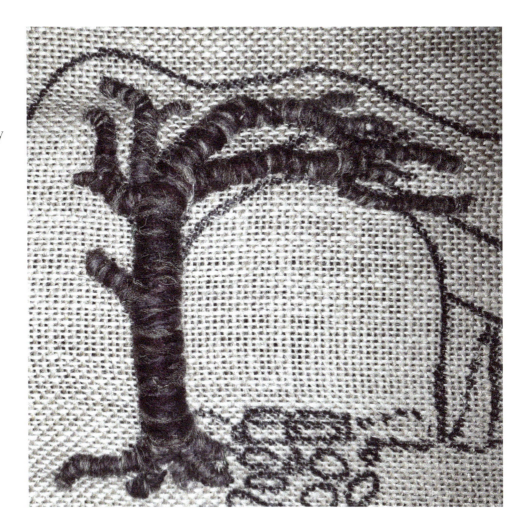

I hooked some leaves around the branches, as though it's fall and the tree has lost some of its leaves. I added some gold leaves to the grassy area when I hooked the rest of the piece.

Here is the hooked piece. As you can see, I haven't added the door yet, that I hooked separately.

Once again, I used the cotton quilt batting to make the grassy area stick up.

(left)
I hemmed down all the edges, and added a couple of the Lincoln locks that we used for Ivy the Sheep to the chimney.

(below)
1. The door is hooked (but not the doorknob).
2. I hemmed the door, trimming away the excess.
3. Using T-shirt material, I sewed on a backing.
4. Sewed on a brass button doorknob.

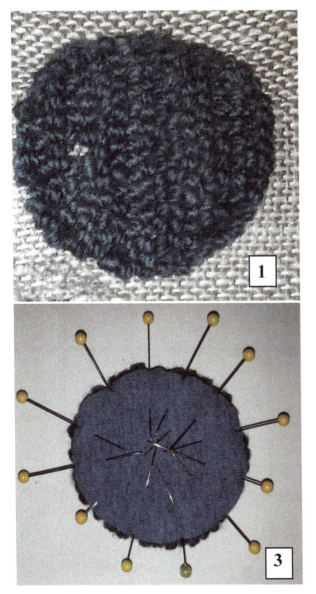

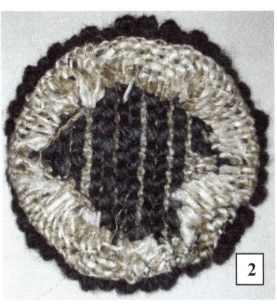

(above) I sewed the door to the hooked piece, then marked the foam board for the back. Ideally, you want the foam board to be slightly smaller than the hooked piece.

(below) I tacked the top of the grassy area to the foam board, as we did with Mischief. I didn't need to tack down the rest of the trapunto; that would get sewn to the backing fabric later.

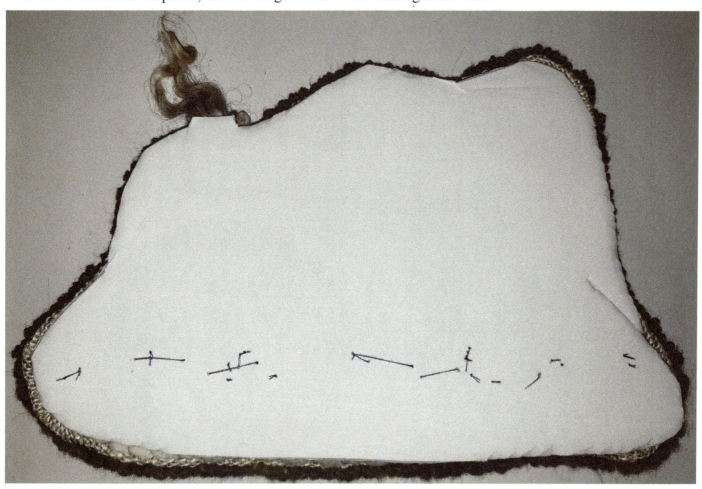

I cut a piece of T-shirt material for the back (above) and sewed it to the hooked mat (below).

I sewed a ring into the back for hanging. To find the right spot, I pushed a needle into the piece and held it up. I moved the needle around as needed to find the place that would allow it to hang straight.

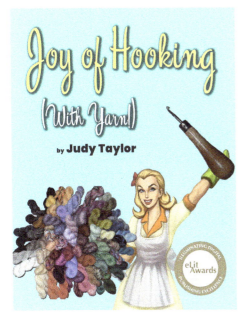

Joy of Hooking (With Yarn!)

All the basics on hooking with yarn are covered; what yarns work best for rug hooking, transferring your designs, building your own frame, etc. Includes easy beginner projects.

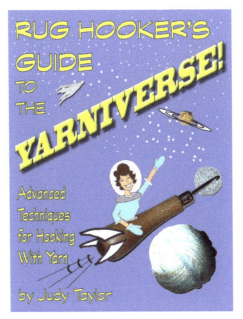

Rug Hooker's Guide to the YARNIVERSE!

Everything beyond the basics; hooking shading and fine detail, primitives, natural colors, multiple dyeing techniques. Includes templates for many projects designed to broaden your skills.

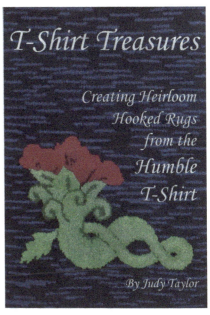

T-Shirt Treasures- Creating Heirloom Hooked Rugs from the Humble T-Shirt

All the basics on hooking durable, inexpensive, machine washable rugs with T-shirts. Includes easy beginner projects.

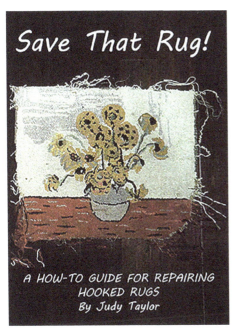

Save That Rug! A How-To Guide for Repairing Hooked Rugs

Everything you need to know to repair old hooked rugs. Hundreds of illustrations and step-by-step instructions.

The photos in this book were taken by Sharon Johnston, Mandy Johnston, John Vickers, Collectors Gallery, Eileen Hordyk, Judy and Gary Taylor.

I would also like to thank Romana Kaspar-Kraft, R. John Howe, Paula Laverty, Elizabeth Herbert, Eileen Hordyk and of course, Sharon Johnston.

Judy Taylor has been teaching and rug hooking for nigh onto thirty years. She is the administrator of Rug Hooking Daily (a free, online rug hooking community with over ten thousand members from all over the world. rughookingdaily.ning.com); as well as a shepherd and handspinner. Her rugs, kits and supplies can be found at www.littlehouserugs.com.

Check out her YouTube videos: Search "Hooking Rugs With Yarn," and "Rug Hooking With T-Shirts."

CPSIA information can be obtained
at www.ICGtesting.com
Printed in the USA
JSHW052015240321
12842JS00005B/2

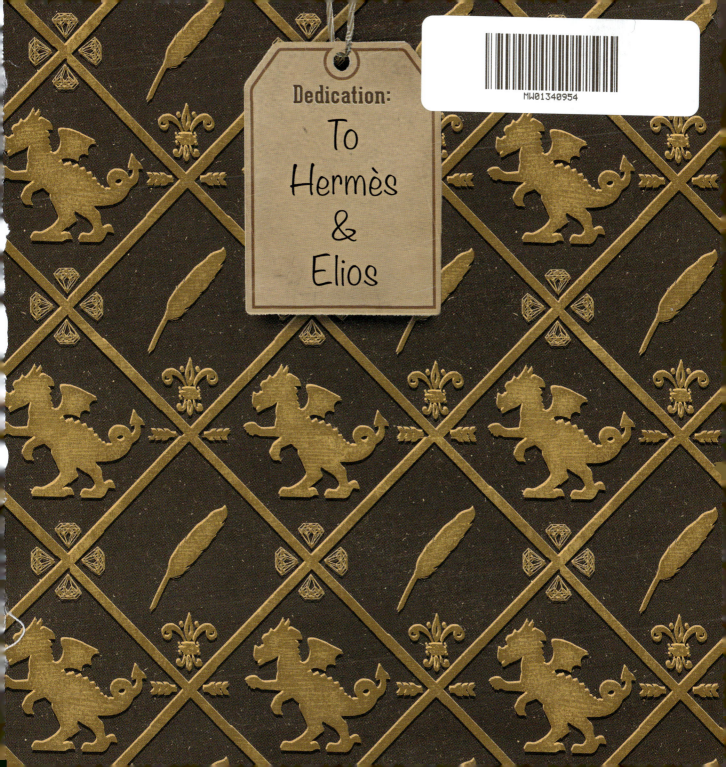

Dedication:
To Hermès & Elios

DRAGONS ARE REAL

Text copyright © 2016 Valarie Budayr
Illustration copyright © 2016 Michael Welply

All rights reserved. No part of this book may be reproduced, transmitted, or stored in an information retrieval system in any form or by any means, graphic, electronic, or mechanical, including photocopying, taping, and recording, without prior written permission from the publisher.

Editor: Roscoe Welply
Art Direction & Design: Roscoe Welply
Lettering: Roscoe Welply

eISBN 978-1-936426-21-8
pISBN 978-1-936426-20-1
Library of Congress info on file.

Printed by Signature Book Printing (www.sbpbooks.com).

This book was hand-lettered by Roscoe Welply.

Audrey Press
P.O. Box 6113
Maryville, TN 37802
Visit us at www.audreypress.com

AudreyPress

Dragons Are Real

Written by Valarie Budayr

Illustrated by Michael Welply

Draco Igneum

I bet you think you know the TRUTH about REAL DRAGONS.

You don't!

I'm sure you've heard in fairy-tales, myths, and legends that dragons breathe fire as they fly about their victims, wiping out entire villages in one fiery breath.

WRONG!

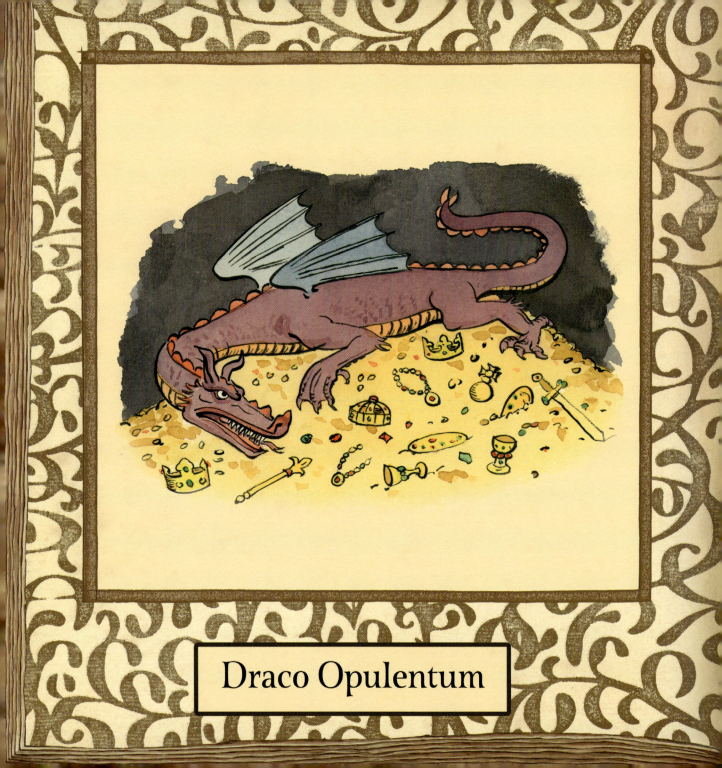

Draco Opulentum

Draco Tyrannicum

I suppose you believe that dragons hoard gold, silver, and other precious trinkets under a magic spell in their caves.

NOPE!!!

You probably also think that dragons fly to and fro looking for "DAMSELS IN DISTRESS" to bring back to their caves. Maybe you've even heard that they eat these distressed damsels with ketchup and mustard on them.

Not TRUE!

The most important thing you should know about REAL DRAGONS is this. Turn the page and never forget what is coming next.

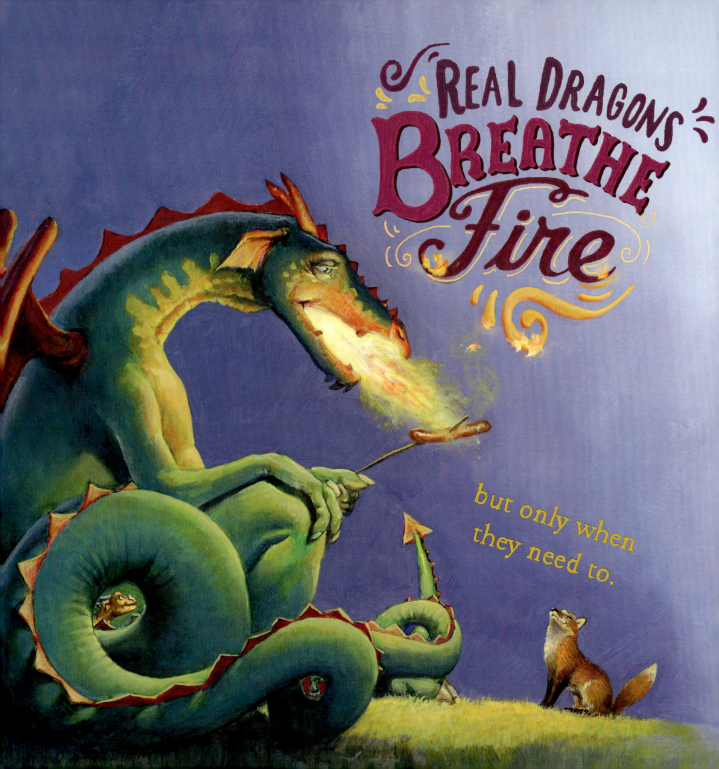

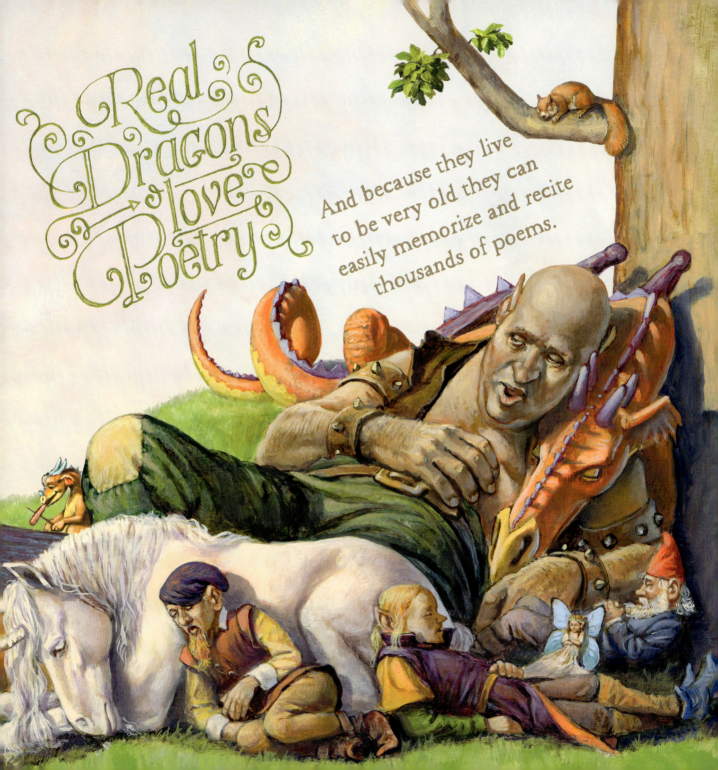

REAL DRAGONS LOVE TO READ

They are extreme hoarders of books. Once you loan a REAL DRAGON a favorite book, consider it a gift because you'll never see it again. Unless, of course, you visit a REAL DRAGON...

In that case I'm sure he'll ask you to sit down and read it with him.

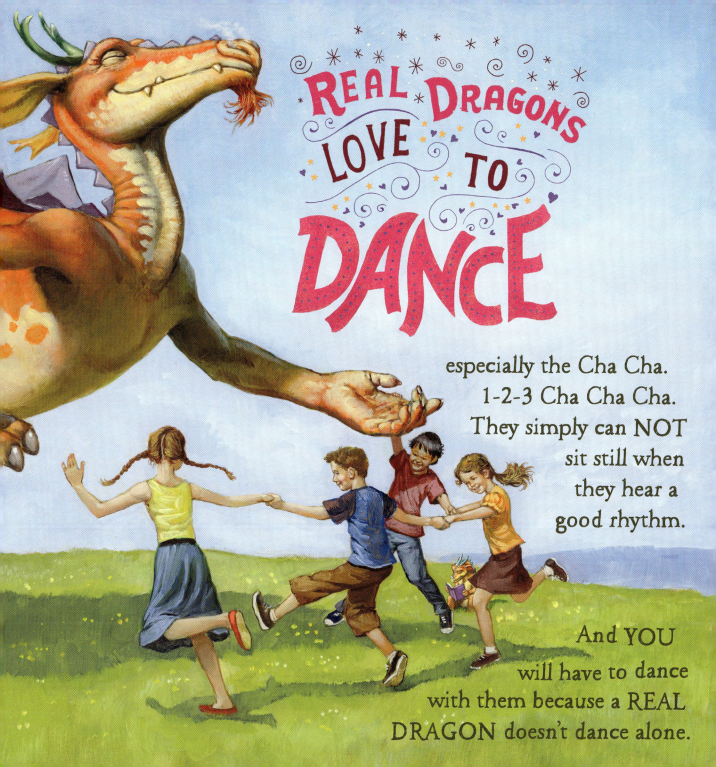

Though it is thought that dragons are vicious and aggressive monsters, nothing could be further from the truth.

REAL DRAGONS LOVE TO LAUGH

REAL DRAGONS are peaceful creatures who just happen to be VERY TICKLISH. If you tickle a dragon on his belly he will snort, kajort, and galumph his way into a hysterical laughing fit.

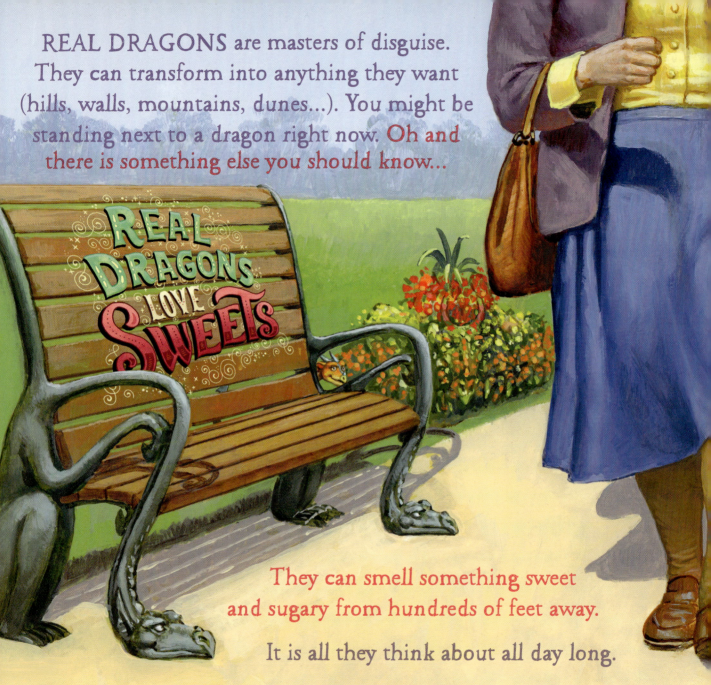

REAL DRAGONS are masters of disguise. They can transform into anything they want (hills, walls, mountains, dunes...). You might be standing next to a dragon right now. Oh and there is something else you should know...

They can smell something sweet and sugary from hundreds of feet away.

It is all they think about all day long.

Their mind will always be whirring, churning, scheming and thinking of a clever disguise for their next big "sweet" abduction.

So if ever one day some of your sweets go missing,
you can be sure that a REAL DRAGON was nearby...

Real dragons love to tell RIDDLES

Better yet they enjoy solving riddles.

The next time you see a REAL DRAGON,
share this riddle and I promise you that
you'll have a REAL DRAGON friend for life.

WHAT MAKES THIS SOUND?

"WHOOSH,...WHOOSH,....WHOOSH,... AH....OOOPS."

ANSWER: A DRAGON PRACTICING HIS JUGGLING.

So from sea to shining sea, somewhere out there right now is a REAL DRAGON waiting to borrow your book, eat your ice cream, recite you a poem, turn into a sand dune for you to roll down, roast your marshmallows, solve a riddle, laugh when he's tickled, but mostly somewhere out there is a REAL DRAGON just waiting to be your next very best friend.

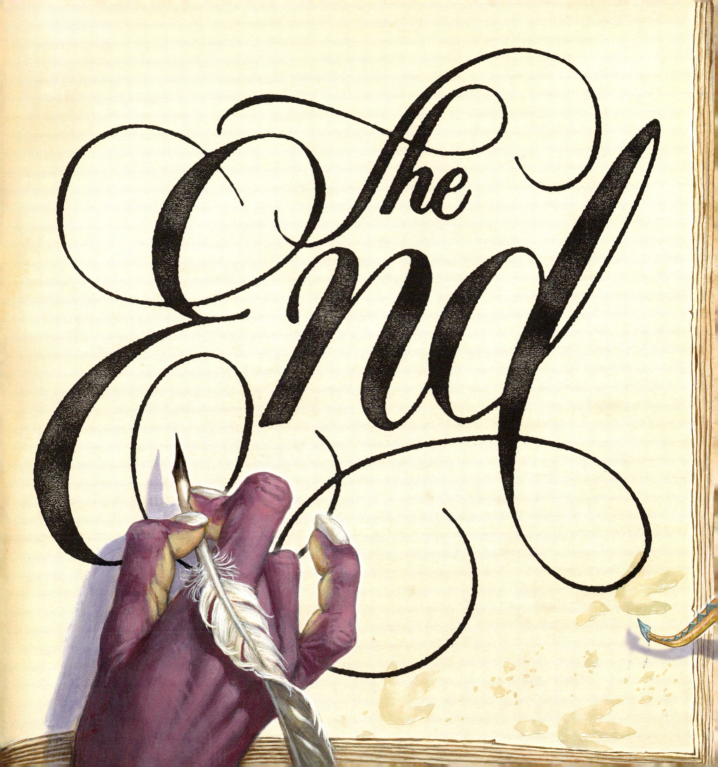

Valarie Budayr loves reading and bringing books alive. Her popular website, www.jumpintoabook.com, inspires children and adults alike to experience their books through play, discovery, and adventure. She is founder of Audrey Press, an independent publishing house as well as an Amazon and iTunes best-selling author. She has written "The Fox Diaries: The Year the Foxes Came to our Garden", "The Ultimate Guide to Charlie and the Chocolate Factory" and "A Year in the Secret Garden". Valarie is co-founder of Multi-cultural Children's Book Day, #ReadYourWorld, a celebration of diverse and cultural kid-lit shared with over 98 million people on January 27th. Her foundation puts hundreds of books into the hands of children in rural intercity areas. www.multiculturalchildrensbookday.com

Michael Welply was born in London, England and raised in Winnipeg, Canada. He studied art in Winnipeg and Paris. He has illustrated over 80 books in Europe and in North America, ranging from historical work to fantasy and fairy tales.

He has two grown children, three grandchildren and currently lives in central France with his wife.

You can find out more about him and see samples of his work on his website: www.michaelwelply.com

www.jumpintoabook.com

info@audreypress.com

www.audreypress.com

Maryville, TN, 37802

PO Box 6113,